KU-004-134

Connections

Ron McKenzie

HODDER AND STOUGHTON
LONDON SYDNEY AUCKLAND TORONTO

Acknowledgments

The author would like to thank Seonaid, Simon and Sarah for comments and for featuring in and/or taking the photographs. For permission to reproduce the photographs in this book the author and publishers would like to thank the following: Ace Photo Agency (p. 29), Butlin's Holidays Ltd (pp. 1 and 35), Christian Aid (p. 86), Scottish Information Office (p. 68), Tony Stone Photolibrary (p. 55), Topham Picture Library (p. 24).

ISBN 0 340 38990 7

First published 1987

Copyright © 1987 Ron McKenzie

All rights reserved. No part of this publication may be reproduced or transmitted in any form or by any means, electronic or mechanical, including photocopy, recording, or any information storage and retrieval system, without permission in writing from the publisher or under licence from the Copyright Licensing Agency Limited. Further details of such licences (for reprographic reproduction) may be obtained from the Copyright Licensing Agency Limited, of 7 Ridgmount Street, London WC1E 7AE.

Printed in Great Britain
for Hodder and Stoughton Educational
a division of Hodder and Stoughton Ltd, Mill Road, Dunton Green, Sevenoaks, Kent by Biddles Ltd, Guildford and King's Lynn

Photoset by Rowland Phototypesetting Ltd, Bury St Edmunds, Suffolk.

Contents

Author's Note

This book has been prepared in the light of the following points.

A reader brings not only reading skills but also his own experience to bear upon the reading task. It is recognised that competence in reading can be demonstrated in the reader's ability to react and respond to the printed word in a variety of ways. These include answering questions on passage content, responding affectively and participating in an enjoyable and productive way in development activities related to the reading passage and enabling the reader to bring his own experience as well as his reading skills to bear. It is also recognised that interest, learning and progress are enhanced if the pupil can relate personally to the reading tasks, if they reflect his own experience, and if he can see that they have an interesting purpose both inherently and in their related developments activities.

Additionally, many teachers believe that a 'shared experience' approach to the teaching of reading including teacher-led group discussion and working with partners, or in groups, facilitates progress. The shared experience can make more meaningful and less difficult the language activities the pupils might go on to whether individually or in a group.

The exercises and activities based on the reading and listening passages are designed to provide experience in the three other language modes, Writing, Listening and Speaking, to give the reader the opportunity to react in a personal way and from his own experience and to engage him in practical activity. The work can be done individually or through the shared experience of prior discussion and group work.

Who needs all that Hi-de-Hi stuff?

Read the story carefully then answer the questions

Here is one of the discussions held by the Watson family, Mike
and Maureen, and their children Peter (15) and Alison (12),
about their forthcoming holiday. (Maybe you have taken part in
a similar discussion with your own family.)

'Oh! Who needs all that Hi-de-hi stuff?' grumbled Mike. 'It's a holiday I want, not a fortnight of obstacle courses at a holiday camp!'

He had been grumbling most of the evening.

5   'Come, Dad, you know it isn't like that,' said Peter. 'Things have changed. It's all self-catering now—very much go as you please—really good evening entertainment with top names from showbiz and all that. Anyway they're called holiday VILLAGES now—not camps.'

10   'Yes, Dad, don't be so stubborn,' Alison spoke up. 'Holiday villages are great fun. You are always telling us about when you were a teenager and went with your pals. Remember?'

'Maybe he's feeling his age,' Peter said.

Mike had to grin but Maureen wagged a finger at the kids.

15   'Pete! Ali! That's no way to talk to your Father!'

There followed a few moments' silence. The four of them were surrounded by brochures advertising hotels, holiday villages, caravan parks, barge and canvas holidays and they had been disagreeing for weeks about which to choose.

20 However, since tea time, it seemed to have narrowed down to hotels, claiming to specialise in family holidays, and holiday villages. Pete and Ali favoured the latter, Mike favoured the former, on the grounds that it would mean a lot less domestic work for Maureen while she, in her easy-going way, was quite

25 unconcerned.

It was Maureen who broke the silence.

'Let's look again at the place Dad was talking about then at some of Pete's choices and see if we can't make up our minds tonight. It'll soon be too late to write away if we don't.'

30   She took a smart looking leaflet from Mike's hand and began reading aloud.

'Chumley's Hotel,' she paused. 'Nice name—and a nice looking place too by its photo.'

She went on.

35   '"We specialise in family holidays offering something for everyone. The spacious grounds—20 acres of woods and meadows provide relaxing walks and three nature trails. The games facilities include two full-size tennis courts, a nine-hole golf course, a well-equipped play area for toddlers and an

40 adventure playground."'

Maureen paused again. Her eyes ran rapidly down the page.

'Inside there's a sauna, a pool, sunbeds, snooker and a mini gym. These are all extra, though. All rooms have colour
45 TV and a bath. Also easy access for invalids and elderly people. Sounds good.'

Pete suppressed a desire to make another wise crack about his Dad. Instead he seized the brochure he had read so often over the past few weeks that he could repeat the contents by
50 heart.

'Listen to this!' he cried. 'This is far better! "Skepton Manor Holiday Village is a superior medium-sized chalet park in the grounds of Skepton Manor with every facility a discerning holiday maker could want. The chalets, self-catering only, are
55 that bit more spacious and are exceptionally well appointed with 2 or 3 bedrooms, lounge with separate dining and cooking area. Large fridge and colour TV are included as are crockery and bed linen."'

Pete looked up. Ali smiled at him, nodding her head
60 encouragingly. Pete read on.

'The Olympic-size swimming pool has a resident coach and instructor. Tennis lessons are available, free, daily at the courts. A bowling green and putting green are provided for the more leisurely inclined while the children will enjoy Skepton's
65 famous Silver sands only 300 yards away down the cliff walk. For the more enthusiastic there are daily guided estuary and inland walks of varying lengths, and for horse lovers, pony trekking every morning from nine to twelve.

The ballroom of the manor house has been converted into
70 a comprehensive fitness and games area offering everything from weight training to chess, all at no extra charge. A well-stocked shop and launderette are also in the house.'

Again Pete looked up, this time at his Dad who was looking thoughtful. Before Mike could respond, Ali said as persuasively
75 as she could,

'I think Pete is right! What else could we want? Skepton Manor has everything—swimming for Pete and me, tennis and country walks for you and Mum. And, we can all help with the chores!'
80 Maureen raised an eyebrow at this, while Mike went on looking thoughtful.

'Well,' he mused, 'it certainly sounds good, does the chalet park. Can't say I'm convinced though!'

The children groaned out loud while Maureen tutted. She

85 reached for the calculator, tapped the buttons for a while and got an answer. She wrote it down, cleared the read-out and fed in some more figures.

'For the four of us, a fortnight at the holiday village would be £265 less than at the hotel,' she said.

90 Mike suddenly looked convinced. He stretched his legs and put his hands behind his head.

'Have I ever told you,' he said, 'about the great holiday camp I went to in 1959?'

A In your notebook

1 Here are the main happenings in the story. Put them into the proper order.

(a) The choice narrows down to hotel or holiday village.
(b) A final decision is taken.
(c) Lengthy discussion begins.
(d) The brochures are sent for.
(e) A comparison between hotel and holiday villages takes place.
(f) Tempers get a little frayed.

2 The family has given quite a lot of thought to this holiday. Find at least two pieces of information which support this.

3 Why do you think Alison said 'Don't be so stubborn Dad'? Find two reasons.

4 Explain the meaning of these phrases *as they are used* in the story:

obstacle courses	(line 2)
self-catering	(line 6)
feeling his age	(line 13)
specialise in	(line 21)
easy-going	(line 24)
easy access for elderly people and invalids	(line 45)
well appointed	(line 55)

5   Make your own choice between the hotel or the holiday village. Now write down two reasons from the passage for your choice and one reason completely your own.

6   The family are all expressing OPINIONS in their discussion. For example 'This is far better', says Peter about Skepton holiday village. That is his OPINION but it is open to argument.
    Look in turn at what the other three people have to say and write down an opinion stated by each one.

7   FACTS are not open to argument. For example, it is a fact (in our story) that Skepton mansion itself contains a games area.
    Look in turn at what the four people have to say and see if you can quote from each an undeniable FACT.

For discussion

8   Why did Peter 'suppress a desire to make another wise crack about his Dad'? What do you think Peter was going to say before he suppressed his desire?

9   The term HOLIDAY VILLAGE is now widely used in preference to HOLIDAY CAMP since it is a more appropriate term. Do you think it is? Justify your point of view.

10   The Watson family are all quite fit but Maureen says 'Easy access for elderly people and invalids'. Why do you think she mentioned that?

11   What do you think was going through Maureen's mind when she 'raised an eyebrow' (line 80)?

12   Do you think the Watsons chose to go to the holiday village? Justify your answer by quoting your clues from the passage.

13   If the passage were to go on, what do you think the next two sentences would be?

In this exercise you will show your ability to be persuasive

You have been away on different kinds of holidays with your family and you have suggested amid groans from the rest of them that the family should now try a holiday village.

Can you make a really convincing case for 2 weeks at a holiday village? Have a try.

1 Complete this list of 'THINGS IN FAVOUR' by thinking up the missing items.
   (a) All entertainments free.
   (b)
   (c) Self-catering if you wish.
   (d)
   (e) Babysitting available.
   (f)
   (g)
   (h) Lots to do outdoors.

2 Award 1, 2, 3 to the items you think would do most to convince *your* family and say why.

3 Put a ? at the two items which are not really very convincing. What are you going to say to your family if they question these ones?

4 Present your argument a bit at a time to the rest of your group to see if you can convince them that it really is worth going to a holiday village for a change.

Holiday camps used to be famed for their WAKEY, WAKEY call first thing in the morning. The greeting was supposed to cheer everyone up (no matter the weather) and inform campers of special events that day.

Pretend that you are the entertainments officer, and write up a list of events which you will try to read out cheerfully even although when you switched on the microphone it had already been raining cats and dogs for an hour.

WHAT are you going to say and HOW are you going to say it?

Put on your little show for the rest of the class and invite them to give you a mark out of ten!

Read this advertisement for a holiday village

D

East Anglia

SKEPTON MANOR HOLIDAY VILLAGE

Spacious chalets—sleep 4–6 people—well appointed. Attractive seaside setting close to beautiful English countryside. Numerous activities available and excellent on site facilities. £120–£140 per week high season. Few vacancies June 29th–August 17th. Further information on request.

---

1 Suppose *your* family were thinking of booking at Skepton Manor holiday village, do you think this advert tells you enough?

2 Keep the needs of your family at the front of your mind and put down what the advert tells you and what you still need to know before you can judge clearly whether Skepton would be suitable. Organise it on the page like this to make a table of information.

What the advert tells me	What I still need to know
Prices Chalets big enough	Our dates available? What are the facilities?

3 Now, use your table of information and write a letter asking for the further information and making enquiries about what *you* need to know.

The sixth day

Read the story carefully then answer the questions.

Despondently, Peter watched the postman go right past the house for the fifth time since the day of the interview. 'You'll hear from us within a week,' the man had said and now five days had passed. Peter tried not to feel desperate and to cheer himself up a bit thought back over what had happened since he left school. It had not really been too bad he supposed. Certainly it had been much better than what some of his school pals had had to go through.

He had left school 12 months before, although the guidance teacher had advised against it, with 7 'O' grades, all of them quite good grades too. He had written over twenty letters of application for jobs and although no offers had been made some of those that did reply said that he had good subject passes to start a course in mechanical engineering. One or two replies had even invited him to re-apply a year later. He had avoided the training schemes at first. 'Slave labour, that's what it is,' was what one of his school friends had said but finally, hanging about doing nothing had proved too much for Peter. He had completed a short course in the intervening months and felt glad he had taken it. His family had been helpful too and his parents, although they could have used the extra income, counselled him against taking what his Mum had called 'just anything'.

Then his luck had turned. He had received a letter about a fortnight before inviting him to an interview a week later for a position as an apprentice engineer. During that week he experienced every state of mind from rock hard confidence to jelly-kneed fear. He had chewed himself think things over. 'I've got to be lucky this time,' said one inner voice. 'Don't count on it. You're only one of hundreds applying,' cautioned another. 'You'd better be thinking about the questions you might get asked,' declared a third. He had even wondered if he might be strong enough for engineering and more than once had flexed his biceps in front of the mirror just to make sure.

He had enjoyed the interview, though it seemed to last a long time. He and 9 other lads of the same age had been shown round the factory by the chief instructor who had described the processes briefly. Peter found he could understand what was going on and, unlike the others, did not find the noise at all disturbing. In the afternoon they had all undergone a short exam in arithmetical calculations and another in which they were required to recognise, name and describe the uses for various tools. Peter had had no trouble with either. Later a group of three men, one of them the chief instructor, and a woman, from various departments, had asked questions about a variety of things: school, hobbies and sports, health and what not, and they seemed interested in his answers. Suddenly it was all over, and he had gone home with growing confidence.

The letter arrived on the sixth day and Peter's 'Yippee' could be heard all over town. Start on Monday! Four days! £68 weekly! The family were full of congratulations. They were also full of advice.

'Think about bus fares. Try to get some kind of season ticket,' said his Mum. 'Money doesn't go as far as you think.' 'I'd go on my bike if I were you,' said his sister. 'He'd better buy an alarm clock so he gets up in time,' said his grandfather to his father. 'You know what youngsters are when it comes to punctuality.' 'A packed lunch would be best,' Mum said to Peter who had been thinking of using the canteen. 'Remember that £2 you owe me,' chimed in his sister.

Peter refrained from putting his hands over his ears and smiled at his family instead. Some of their advice was on the button though. Tonight after tea he would give thought to all these things and make a budget. He would need to buy a few things for work and although he had not let on to his family, he wanted to get them all a little something with his first pay.

 ## In your notebook

1   Here are some of the happenings in the story. Put them into the correct order.

(a) The family gives Peter plenty of advice.
(b) He does the exams in arithmetic and tool recognition.
(c) He leaves school.
(d) He decides to make a budget for spending his pay.
(e) He receives the letter offering him a job.
(f)   He applies repeatedly for jobs.

2   Draw and complete this table. The first one is done for you but check it anyway.

Number of the paragraph	What the paragraph is mainly about
Paragraph 1	'Peter is waiting anxiously for a letter.'
Paragraph 3 Paragraph 4 Paragraph 6 Paragraph 7	

3 Why do you think Peter felt 'desperate' when the postman passed for the fifth consecutive day?

4 Peter's guidance teacher advised against his leaving school. Why do you think the teacher did this?

5 A school friend called the training schemes 'slave labour' which is his OPINION and not a FACT. Find 2 other examples of stated OPINIONS in the story.

For discussion

6 Why should Peter have felt glad that he completed the short training course?

7 What is the meaning of Mum's phrase 'just anything'? Why does she use it?

8 Peter went home 'with growing confidence'. Do you think he was right to feel confident? Say why.

9 Peter must have been a good candidate for the apprenticeship. Complete this table of possible reasons as far as you can.
   (a) He had good 'O' grades
   (b)
   (c)
   (d)
   (e)
   (f)

10 Why should the panel ask Peter about school, hobbies and sports?

11 What do you think of Peter's antics in front of the mirror?

12 Why might Mum say that a packed lunch would be best? Give two reasons that Mum might have.

13 Continue this list of things that Peter would need to be thinking about now that he has a job.

> The best way to get to work
> Whether to use the canteen

Give each item a rating from 1 to 10 to show its importance. Give a reason why you have rated the highest one so highly. Give a reason for rating the lowest one so low.

1   Money to throw away?

Peter is soon to get his first pay and has already begun to draw up a budget, to which we may be sure he will give a great deal of thought.

Suppose you had just got your first pay packet and say it was £68 for working a 6-day week in a sports shop.

    (a) Write in your notebook a list of the things you need the money for or are going to spend it on.
Start like this

Fares	*4.80*
Lunches	*6.60*

and end like this

Savings	*???*

    (b) Rearrange your list so that the most important things are at the top.
    (c) Put opposite each item the amount of money that it is to get.
    (d) See if somehow you can make it total up to no more than £68.

2   A head start?

Completing the training scheme probably helped Peter to get his job.

What can you find out about these schemes? Here is how to go about finding out.

(a) Ask older boys and girls in your street if they are on a scheme and get them to tell you about it. Ask whether they like it or not, what they do and what they hope to do once the course is over.

(b) Write a letter to the local job centre asking for leaflets about the schemes, and make a display or scrapbook of the leaflets.

(c) Make notes about the schemes for a short talk to the rest of the class.

3 Now think about yourself

(a) When you get a job, which would you prefer—an outdoor job or an indoor one? Complete these tables.

An outdoor job is GOOD because	An outdoor job is NOT SO GOOD because
An indoor job is GOOD because	An indoor job is NOT SO GOOD because

(b) What job do you want to do when you are 'grown up'? Write a paragraph saying what your choice of job is and why you have chosen it.

(c) Have you ever waited anxiously for a letter? Perhaps it was about getting a Saturday job; perhaps it contained something you sent away for; perhaps it was from someone you had met on holiday who had promised to write; perhaps it was none of these and was something else instead.

Write a few paragraphs about why you waited anxiously, what went through your mind and how things turned out when it finally arrived.

It does you good

Sports in Seaborough 1985

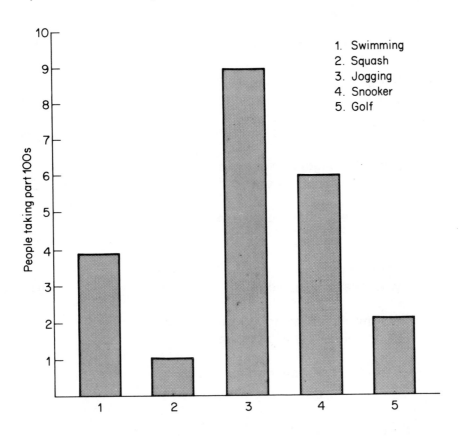

1. Swimming
2. Squash
3. Jogging
4. Snooker
5. Golf

People taking part 100s (y-axis)

Here is a graph for the year 1985 showing the numbers of people taking part in 5 sports available in Seaborough and its surrounding area.

Read the graph.

In your notebook

Write down the sports in a list and put opposite each the number of people who took part.

What is the graph telling us?

Put a ring round T or F or DS to show TRUE, FALSE or the graph DOESN'T SAY.

1	Jogging was the most popular.	T	F	DS
2	Twice as many people played golf played squash.	T	F	DS
3	Golf is the least popular sport.	T	F	DS
4	Every teenager and adult in Seaborough took part in a sport of some kind.	T	F	DS
5	Some people took part in more than one sport.	T	F	DS
6	Jogging was most popular because it was least expensive.	T	F	DS
7	Swimming attracted as many followers as squash and golf put together.	T	F	DS
8	Between them, swimming and golf attracted more people than snooker.	T	F	DS

For discussion

Be prepared to give reasons of your own since the answers are not always on the graph.

9   Clearly *jogging* is the most popular. Why do you think it is?

Here are some possible reasons. Complete the list.

    (a) Available to all ages

    (b)

    (c)

    (d)

    (e)

10 Six times as many people played *snooker* as played *squash*. Again, complete this list of possible reasons.

    (a) There are many more snooker tables than squash courts.

    (b)

    (c)

    (d) Squash is a really tough game.

11 Swimming has a good following. An obvious reason is that it is an all age sport. Give 3 more reasons below.

    (a)

    (b)

    (c)

However swimming is well behind jogging in popularity. Again try to complete this table of reasons why.

    (a)

    (b)

    (c)

    (d)

12 Look at the entry for *squash*. Only about 100 people took part. Certainly, squash tends to be a tough game for really fit younger people but there are surely other reasons. Can you think of them?

13 Golf attracted 200 people—not really very many. It is an expensive game however. Clubs alone can go into hundreds of pounds. But other reasons must also exist. Can you give at least 2?

Make a graph about the sports and pastimes your classmates enjoy. Ask them for the basic information and enter it on a tally sheet like this. (You can complete separate ones for boys and girls.) Then draw a graph similar to the Seaborough graph.

SPORT	NUMBER OF PEOPLE WHO WATCH OR PLAY
FOOTBALL	IHt IHt IHt II
TENNIS	IHt II
SNOOKER	IHt IHt IHt

Now what about YOU?

What is YOUR favourite sport whether you take part in it or only spectate?

Write a short talk to deliver to your classmates. Your talk should include information on:

What your favourite sport is.
Why it is your favourite.
Some information about the sport like where and when it first began.
Where and how often you go to pursue your sport.
What it costs.
Any problems you face trying to keep up your sport.
At least 3 reasons why you think others should become fans.

Try to make your talk last about 5 minutes. Be ready to answer questions and REMEMBER items which the others can *see*, like the equipment used, posters, etc., will make your talk really interesting.

The great hall

Alex stepped through the enormous door of the great hall into the rays of the setting sun streaming through the eight tall windows opposite. He blinked to adjust his eyes to the light inside and looked about him. He was startled at first. He stood stock still. There seemed to be a row of faces peering at him. He grinned, and looked at the line of statues of the Duke and Duchess, their six children and the latter's two grandfathers spaced at regular intervals along the north wall.

Alex ran his gaze away from the statues along the windows, which—apart from the space occupied by what the guide book called the 'great central fireplace'—took up the whole of the wall, right down to the far end to the central stairway which protruded a good fifteen feet out across the floor of the hall. The stairway was really quite majestic as it disappeared upwards into the adjoining part of the castle.

He moved into the centre of the hall to try to see up the staircase, but his view was interrupted by a bulky plinth placed midway between himself and the stair wall. The plinth carried the statue of a horse and rider rearing up in an arrogant posture. Another statue, this time of a Crimean soldier, occupied a similar place towards the other end of the hall.

Around the base of the horseman, their legs standing on the metre wide black and white squares of marble which covered the floor of the hall, were arranged four display cases containing a variety of curios gathered over the centuries. Alex walked towards them stepping on to the extensive Dutch carpet which stretched from the centre of the hall to the edge of the display. He looked for a few moments at medals and pistol butts, daggers and brass and silver buttons, then gazed up at the carved ceiling, marvelling at the sheer enormity of the hall and its deafening silence. The assignment card in Alex's hand instructed him to record 4 facts which would illustrate how large this great room was in comparison with rooms in the Georgian houses in their last project. In addition, he was to write a sentence or two about the one item that had interested him most. He knew what that was—the hidden opening, somewhere in the floor which led to the dungeons below. He folded out his metre ruler and laboriously measured the floor down its whole length. 60 metres long and half as wide. The windows were 5 metres wide and, he guessed, about 6 high. I would not like to clean these on the Scout job week, he thought. He measured the carpet. It was a square—exactly a quarter of the size of the floor he calculated. He discovered that the central fireplace was no less than 6 metres from side to side.

Now, what about that hidden trapdoor? He knelt and searched the large black and white squares carefully without success. He was on the point of rising wearily to his feet when a low voice near him said 'Time to go home, my lad!'.

He looked round and directly in front of the fireplace he saw the trapdoor, and the guide climbing up into view. He had probably been in the dungeons for some reason.

'It's 5.30 now!' the guide continued. 'Time to lock the big doors.'

Read the story carefully then, working with a partner, complete the questions and assignments and draw the plan.

Have you an eye for detail? Can you make use of clues? Discuss these questions and find the answers. Note the answers down. This will help you to draw the plan.

1   As Alex enters the Great Hall, in which direction is he facing, NORTH, SOUTH, EAST or WEST? How do you know?

2   Are the statues on Alex's RIGHT or his LEFT as he enters the Great Hall?

3   The central stairway emerges from the south wall. TRUE or FALSE or DOESN'T SAY?

4   The statue of the horse and rider is situated towards the north end of the Hall. TRUE or FALSE or DOESN'T SAY?

5   The Dutch carpet stretches all the way from the statue of the Crimean soldier to the statue of the horse and rider. TRUE or FALSE or DOESN'T SAY?

6   The ceiling is 10 metres high. TRUE or FALSE or DOESN'T SAY?

7   The Great Hall is much bigger than any of the rooms in the Georgian houses which Alex studied before. TRUE or FALSE or DOESN'T SAY?

8   The distance between the windows is probably about: 3.5 metres, 2.5 metres or 1.5 metres?

As we read the story of the GREAT HALL and what Alex is doing we learn where things are LOCATED.

e.g. The eight tall windows are *OPPOSITE* the enormous door.
The statue of the horse and rider is *MIDWAY BETWEEN* Alex and the stair wall.
The display cases are arranged *AROUND THE BASE* of the horseman.

OPPOSITE, MIDWAY BETWEEN, AROUND THE BASE, are LOCATION words and phrases because they give you clues about where the various items are situated or LOCATED.

Draw this table and complete it. Some words and phrases are given. Find others for each paragraph.

	Location words and phrases
Para 1	1 opposite 2 3
Para 2	1 *central* fireplace 2 3
Para 3	1 2 similar place 3 towards other end of the hall
Para 4	1 around the base 2 edge of the display 3
The rest of the story	1 near him 2 3

Complete this list of objects and features that you would show on a plan of the GREAT HALL.

    1 Door
    2 Eight windows
    3
    4 Central fireplace
    5
    6 Statue of Crimean soldier
    7
    8
    9 Black and white marble squares
   10

Any more?

Now, with your partner use the information gained from A, B and C to draw a plan of the GREAT HALL showing all the features of interest, and using words or symbols to represent them.

You will need: a sharp pencil
a ruler
a rubber
a large sheet of paper

Start like this.

1 Draw the outline rectangle.

2 Mark NORTH, SOUTH, EAST and WEST on the
appropriate sides.

We are told little or nothing about the dungeons in which Alex
is interested.

The Great Hall has been open to the public for a long time,
and now the dungeons are to be opened too.

Design an information leaflet all about the dungeons to try
to attract tourists and visitors.

The leaflet should contain

A simple plan of the dungeons showing how you imagine
them to be and including all their important features.
A paragraph to go along with the plan describing the
dungeons and the fate of some of their imaginary inmates.

Many people visit stately homes and castles when on holiday,
sometimes because they are genuinely interested and
sometimes only because it is wet yet again. Usually the visits
are enjoyable, but sometimes they are not.

Have you visited a stately home or castle? Why? How did
the visit go?

Write 2 or 3 paragraphs telling how your visit came about,
what you saw, the atmosphere, the kind of people you met,
what in particular you enjoyed and what could have been
altered or improved to appeal more to your own age group. Try
to get some of the leaflets from the visit and stick them in your
notebook along with your paragraphs to make an interesting
account.

A day in the life of Grant

Listen carefully to the story then answer the questions

A In your notebook

Answer questions 1–5 by writing (a), (b), (c) or (d).

1 One hundred yards away from where he came ashore Grant could see

    (a) a crowd of people.
    (b) a group of fishing boats.
    (c) the docks.
    (d) the cliff path.

2 Before he fell asleep Grant
- (a) had a quick wash at the water's edge.
- (b) heard the voices of the teenagers.
- (c) heard the ship's whistle.
- (d) thought about what he had to do.

3 The teenagers were
- (a) arguing about whether or not to swim.
- (b) searching in their bags.
- (c) holding a race to see who would be first in the water.
- (d) finishing their food.

4 Against orders, Grant
- (a) slept for several hours.
- (b) hid so he could watch both the litter bin and the ship.
- (c) tried to remain undetected.
- (d) chose to use the cliff path.

5 When the ship's whistle sounded
- (a) the gang plank was raised.
- (b) a figure came down the gang plank.
- (c) the contact ran towards the ship.
- (d) Grant dropped the package into the litter bin.

6 Here are six things Grant did in the story but they are out of order. Put them into the correct order.
- (a) Climbed the cliff path.
- (b) Decided to remain on the beach.
- (c) Had a much needed sleep.
- (d) Clung to the rocks.
- (e) Went over his plans.
- (f) Stole some food.

7 Explain the meaning of these words and phrases *as they are used* in the story.
- (a) a long comprehensive look
- (b) analysed the situation
- (c) reviewed
- (d) the heat was off
- (e) triggered

8 Why do you think Grant noted that there were 'plenty of footholds and crevices' in the cliff?

9 What is meant by 'use the dogs'?

10 From this list select the two words that you think best describe Grant:

strong   resourceful   lucky   stubborn   brave

What are your reasons for your choice?

11 In the story two groups of people are referred to as 'they'. Say who 'they' are in each case.

B Use the clues you heard while listening to the passage to draw a simple plan of the beach. Put yourself in Grant's position as he stood up on the rocks and took a 'long comprehensive look' around him.

C *For discussion*

12 Do you find it curious that Grant should not know what the package contained? Say why.
    What do you think it contained?

13 Why should Grant think it was wise to 'stay put'?

14 Why should the author use the phrase 'a *gaggle* of teenagers'?

15 Does it strike you as odd that Grant should feel uneasy that no pursuit seemed to have been mounted? Give reasons for your point of view.

16 'Against orders', Grant retreated into the shadows. Why do you think he made up his mind to go against orders?

17 Do you think Grant was right to try to see his contact? How would that have been of use to Grant?

The passage is obviously only one part of the story. A great deal must have gone before and a great deal might come afterwards if Grant is as good at the long jump as we all hope.

Would you like to give the story a beginning and an end?

You can hold a competition among yourselves. Go about it like this.

1   Get a partner to be your co-author.

2   The extract you have just read has three distinct 'parts'. Here they are in flow-chart form.

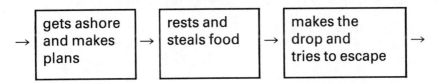

→ | gets ashore and makes plans | → | rests and steals food | → | makes the drop and tries to escape | →

Copy this on to the middle of your notebook page.

3   Make three more rectangles for BEFORE and three more for AFTER.

4   Enter them with the key ideas and review the chart to see if it all hangs together.

5   Fill out the story with a short paragraph for each rectangle on the chart. Share out the work equally.

6   Along with some other pairs, read out your completed story to the class and see whose gets the most applause.

1   Grant does dangerous work suited only to a special kind of person who has special qualities. Think of qualities to complete the list below.

(a)
(b) intelligence
(c)
(d)
(e) courage
(f)

2   If you had all six qualities would you want to be a secret agent? Write a paragraph saying why or why not.

3   A secret agent has to know how to SURVIVE, and many are equipped with a survival kit, which is a set of objects and items each of which is *useful* and *essential*.

Make up a list of six items to form a survival kit for

(a) an agent operating in the Arctic Circle;
(b) yourself to enable you to spend 3 days and nights outside.

Which would be more exciting, (a) or (b)? Why?

Bad times get worse

Read the story carefully and answer these questions.

October 16, 1986
LEE VALLEY ADVERTISER

Bad times get worse!

We should have seen it coming!
by our industrial correspondent

Lee Valley people are paying the price of depending too heavily and for too long on the three old hardies—steel, textiles and furniture. These industries could be relied on to provide steady jobs and steady income in the past, but the worldwide recession is here and demand is right down. Nobody wants (or more probably, can afford) these things or they can be imported cheaply and there is no new industry to fall back on as factory closures and job losses proceed apace. The effects are therefore particularly severe and are being felt by every family.

These effects were first felt in the late sixties and early seventies when the Lee Valley was first faced with difficult problems. The steel works found it hard to sell their steel because other countries, some in the Third World, were producing too much at competitive prices. The same was happening in textiles. Countries in the Far East flooded our markets with inexpensive items of surprisingly good

quality and design. Demand for the solid, long-lasting furniture, for which Lee Valley manufacturers have long
30 been famous, disappeared with the arrival of the cheaper DIY self-assembly kits. The Lee Valley factories and mills began to lose money and orders in a big way.

35 That was bad news for the Valley people. Management, workers and local politicians did their best to grapple with the crisis but no matter what they did, closures occurred and
40 people lost their jobs. Steel was the worst hit. By the end of last year the workforce had dwindled by no less than two-thirds.

Things have inevitably deterio-
45 rated since then. Despite government help, too little too late according to some, there have been no improvements.

But today's news must be the worst yet. Deep shock and bewilder- 50 ment were expressed by all Valley people at the noon announcement that more than seven hundred steel jobs —a massive three-quarters of the remaining workforce—are to disappear 55 at the outset of the summer holiday. The outlook is no longer just bleak. It is desperate. There is no other industry here, and we are left with these empty shells of factories. One wonders why, 60 years ago, no one seemed alert enough to foresee what was going to happen. But it is all so much spilt milk. We have got to face it. The time has come for new ideas, fresh clear thinking and 65 drastic action if the Lee Valley is going to have a future of any kind.

A In your notebook

1 Write down the 3 main industries in the Lee Valley.

2 How many people, approximately, were employed in steel during the early 1960s?

3 The title of the story says 'Bad Times'. From the story give a reason which shows that times were not always bad.

4 Write down three reasons for the times becoming bad.

5 How have these bad times affected the Lee Valley people?

6 Explain the meaning of these phrases as they are used in the passage.

(a)	old hardies	(line 3)
(b)	steady jobs and steady income	(lines 5–6)
(c)	proceed apace	(line 13)
(d)	competitive prices	(line 23)
(e)	in a big way	(line 34)
(f)	too little too late	(lines 46)
(g)	empty shells	(lines 59–60)

For discussion

7   What do you understand by 'the Third World'?

8   Why do you think the writer says 'surprisingly good quality and design'?

9   The word 'inexpensive' is used (lines 25–26) to describe the textile imports. Why did the author not just say 'cheap'?

10 Why does the author say 'dwindled by' rather than 'reduced by'.

11 It says 'management, workers and local politicians did their best'. What do you think they could have done?

12 'But it is all so much spilt milk.' What is the meaning of this curious phrase?

13 Name two other effects of the worldwide recession.

It can happen anywhere

You may work with a partner on these assignments.

1   You have heard the news about a huge forthcoming job loss at an important factory in your area and your newspaper has sent you to interview workers as they leave the factory.

Complete this list of questions you could ask them. Write your questions so that they don't get just a 'Yes' or 'No' answer.

   (a) When did you first hear the news?
   (b)
   (c) What are your prospects of re-employment now?
   (d)
   (e)

2   What would the crowd be like?

   (a) A crowd gathered at the factory at an event like this would be made up of more than just the workers. Make a list of who else was there.

(b) Underline the words which might describe the various moods of the crowd.

resignation, elation, anger, despair, relief, bewilderment.

(c) Now write a 2-paragraph report, for your paper, describing the scene and the atmosphere.

3 Record a short interview between yourself (as the reporter) and a partner (as a worker, either an older person or a newly employed school leaver) to show how they feel and what they are going to do.

4 The shock announcement of the closure of a factory, and the job losses incurred, often make a good news item for radio or television.

Make a short television item for the news programme based on a factory closure. Use this format.

(a) Announcement of closure by *newsreader*.
(b) Interview between *reporter* and *worker*.
(c) Back in the studio the *industrial correspondent* discusses problem briefly with local *MP* or the *factory manager* or the *union official*.

Some notes to help you.
(a) Include the name of the factory, what it makes, the size of the workforce, cause of closure and link phrases to introduce the interview.
(b) Make sure the questions include some about the closure and some relating to the interviewee so he can show his feelings.
(c) The industrial correspondent might give some background information before the discussion began.
   The most important questions might be 'How did it happen?' 'What now?'.

Imagine it happened to you

1 Loss of income to a family nearly always means that they can think of buying only *essential food*. Make a list of the foods you think essential for a family of four (2 adults, 2 children) for one week.

2 Your Dad (or Mum) has just lost his job and has just told the family.

Write 7 or 8 sentences telling what everybody said or did when the news was broken.

3 Your family is going to move elsewhere because a really good job is available. Complete this table.

Things I am going to miss	Things I am looking forward to
1	1
2	2
3	3
4	4
5	5
6	6

Nearly every community in the country has suffered a closure of some kind

Is there a factory or workplace near you going through the same troubled times as the *Lee Valley Advertiser* has been telling us about?

1 Go to the library and look through the local paper for the past year to find the information you need.

2 Read the articles and rewrite one of them as if you had been the reporter on that story.

3 Make a flow chart of events something like this.

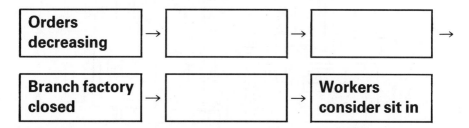

4 Make your own headlines and billboards for a shopfront display.

Skepton Holiday Village

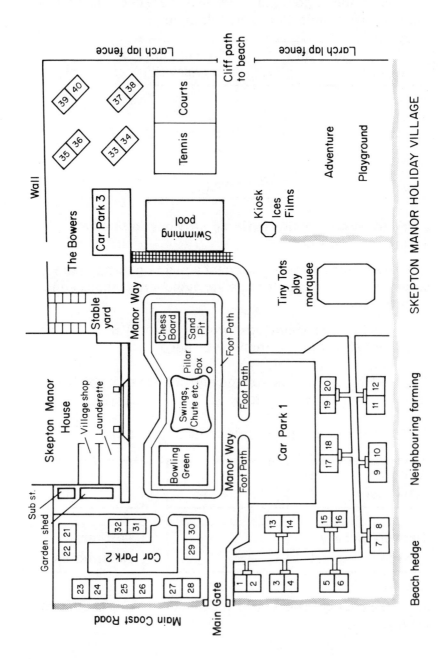

Larch lap fence Cliff path to beach Larch lap fence

Wall

39 40   37 38

35 36   33 34

Tennis   Courts

The Bowers

Car Park 3

Swimming pool

Kiosk
Ices
Films

Adventure

Playground

Stable yard

Manor Way

Chess Board

Sand Pit

Tiny Tots play marquee

Foot Path

Skepton Manor House

Village shop

Launderette

Swings, Chute etc.

Pillar Box

Foot Path

Sub st.

Garden shed

Bowling Green

Manor Way

Foot Path

Car Park 1

19 20

11 12

17 18

9 10

22 21

32 31

29 30

Car Park 2

13 14

15 16

7 8

23 24

25 26

27 28

1 2

3 4

5 6

Main Gate

Main Coast Road

SKEPTON MANOR HOLIDAY VILLAGE

Neighbouring farming

Beach hedge

34

In this exercise you will show your ability to interpret and gain information from a map, and identify and solve problems. Read the descriptive notes about the holiday village and study the map carefully for a while.

Skepton holiday village, in the grounds of SKEPTON MANOR, has accommodation for 200 guests in three groups of chalets for 4 or 6 people.

Outdoor facilities include a bowling green, a swimming pool, two hard tennis courts, the Bowers rose garden, a tiny tots' play marquee, swings and chute area, an adventure playground, an outsize chessboard, ices and films kiosk, a splendid beach and many seaside and country walks. The grounds are laid in luxurious lawns and there is ample car parking for guests and visitors. Pony trekking is available on certain weekdays.

Inside the manor house are the games area, the village shop, the phone booths and a modern launderette.

Use the map to get your answers

1 Where is everything?

Find the three car parks   sand pit
tennis courts   chalet No. 25
village shop   cliff path
bowling green   electricity sub-station
tiny tots' marquee   gardener's shed
chalet No. 16   stable yard

In your notebook

2 Take the PILLAR BOX as the centre of the village, and, in your head, divide the village into 4 quarters like this:

(NW) Top left	(NE) Top right
— centre —	
(SW) Bottom left	(SE) Bottom right

Now do these

(a) The bowling green is in the . . . quarter
(b) The tiny tots' play marquee is in the . . . quarter
(c) Chalet No. 34 is in the . . . quarter
(d) The Manor house is in the . . . quarter
(e) Chalet No. 18 is in the . . . quarter
(f) The outsize chess board is in the . . . quarter

3 (a) Name a facility to the EAST of Chalet No. 20.
(b) What is almost due SOUTH of the Manor's front door?
(c) What is NORTH of car park 3?
(d) Which direction do you take going from the tennis court to the main coast road?
(e) Which direction do you take to go from the swimming pool to the ices kiosk?
(f) Chalets 33–40 lie to the . . . of the swimming pool.
(g) The sand pit lies to the . . . of the adventure playground.

4 Choose a *safe* route.
   (a) Write down directions on how to get from Chalet 16 to Chalet 34.
   (b) Write down directions on how to get from the village shop to the adventure playground.

5 Name 3 places (not including Manor Way) where you think children should mind carefully how they go.

6 Which group of chalets is placed most favourably? Write down as many reasons as possible for your answer.

7 Find chalet 25 which is for 4 people. Like all the others, it will have its advantages and disadvantages arising from where it is placed. Complete this table as far as you can.

CHALET 25	
Advantages	Disadvantages
Close to shop and launderette	Backs on to *main* coast road

Now think about your own family

8 Write down the number of the chalet you like best. Give reasons for your choice.

9 Suppose your family were given Chalet No. 1 for their holiday, do you think they would want to go back to it another year? Explain your answer.

Problem solving

You may work with a partner or in groups and report your findings to the rest of the class.

   The holiday village is clearly a busy place with between 200 and 300 people going about so it needs to be SAFE, TIDY and CONVENIENT.

1   Make a list of the facilities available to everybody like this

BOWLING GREEN   KIOSK
SWIMMING POOL   . . .
TENNIS COURTS   . . .

and give each one a *location rating* like this

√√   (very well located)
√   (well located)
?   (poorly located)
??   (very poorly located)

Now select two of *your* best ones and give 3 reasons for each explaining why you have rated them highly.

With two facilities which you rated poorly give reasons why, suggest how you would improve things, or where you would prefer to locate the facilities anyway.

2   Suggest 2 locations where you would put a pedestrian crossing as a safety precaution, starting with the more urgent.

For each crossing write 2 or 3 reasons why you want it put there.

3   The chalets all have waste bins but litter bins are needed throughout the village.

Choose six locations where they are needed and write the places in a list.

Number the list in order of 'most needed' to 'least needed' and give a reason explaining your choice of location.

4   While the chalets are well appointed, there is no PUBLIC toilet shown on the map.

If you think one is necessary find a suitable location for it, saying why you think the location suitable.

If you think a public toilet is unnecessary give a number of reasons for your opinion.

5   Some people might think a 'meeting' or 'rallying' point in the village would be useful. Choose a location for one which is fairly easy to get to but would not inconvenience guests using the various facilities. Explain your choice of location.

6 More money is going to be spent on the village and the possible new facilities are:
- a small amusement arcade for 20 machines
- a crazy golf course
- a film house with video films
- a set of climbing frames and plastic animals in each chalet area (for the small children)
- ramps and rails throughout the village for invalid access.

Select the two facilities you think would be of most benefit to guests and explain why you have selected them.
State where you would locate the new facilities and say why.

7 You have had an enjoyable holiday before at Skepton with a pal and her parents, but your family has never been until this year. You want them to enjoy their stay as much as possible so see if you can plan at least their first day's activities for them. Remember the family does not have to be together all day. Here is how you can do it.

(a) Make a list of all the activities available at Skepton. Number the activities 1, 2, 3, 4 and so on, like this

SWIMMING	1
TENNIS	2
BOWLING	3
BEACH	4
	5
	6
	and so on

(b) Copy and complete this table.

Family member	2 favourite activities	
Mum	1	4
Dad	2	4
Gran		
Self		
Brother		
Sister		

(c) Now make up a day's 'timetable' for them using a table like the one above and including MORNING, AFTERNOON and EVENING.

It's a dog's life

In 'IT'S A DOG'S LIFE' there are three different kinds of reading to do—an *extract from an official report, a graph,* and *some poetry* written by young people at school. All three deal with the same subject but each delivers its own message in its own special way. See what you think of them.

Read this extract from the report

1985 had more bad aspects than good. More cases than ever were investigated by our inspectors—up from 550 the previous year to 640. However, proportionately more offenders were punished. Of these 640 cases, more than three-quarters
5 concerned domestic pets suffering neglect, cruelty or abandonment. By far the greater part of that 75% was made up by cases concerning dogs. Generally, the dogs were found wandering, distressed, starving, injured and pest-ridden. To make matters worse during this past year, not nearly so many
10 people have felt able to offer a good home to abandoned pets. Perhaps we can blame this on the present economic climate. More positively, our researchers have discovered that, although in general fees have gone up, conditions and standards in the country's boarding kennels have continued to
15 improve. Domestic pets are still wandering on to major roads, according to police records, and during the last quarter of the year there were more reports of stray dogs running in packs through housing estates in a number of our major towns. The experiment with dog warden teams, however, has begun to
20 contribute to the alleviation of this problem.
　　　Volunteers and helpers, of which there is always a huge supply in our schools, deserve heartfelt thanks.

A　*For discussion*

1　Give the meanings of these words and phrases *as they are used in the report*.

proportionately	(line 3)
generally	(line 7)
more positively	(line 12)
alleviation	(line 20)

2　A number of groups of people who contribute to the welfare of animals are referred to in the story. Complete this list.

(a)　inspectors (from the society)
(b)
(c)
(d)
(e)
(f)
(g)

3   What does the inspector mean when he says 'perhaps we can blame this on the present economic climate' (line 11)?

4   Can you give reasons from your own experience to suggest why 'more cases than ever' had to be 'investigated'?

5   What kinds of things do you think the dog wardens in our story did in the course of their work?

B   **Study this graph which gives information about dogs in one dog refuge.**

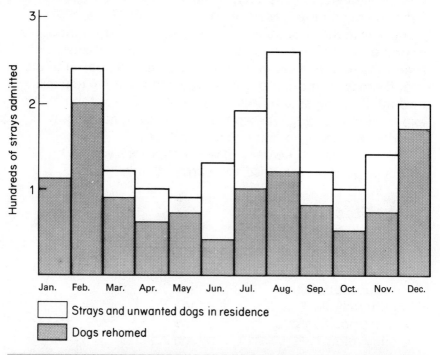

Strays and unwanted dogs in residence

Dogs rehomed

For discussion

1   Which 4 months are 'worst' in the sense that most strays were admitted? Give reasons why these should be the worst months.

2   In December 200 stray dogs were admitted but no less than 170 were rehomed. What do you think is the reason for this encouraging fact?

3 July and August seem to be fairly good months for rehoming the dogs. Why, do you think, this should be?

4 Non-availability of a new home is only one reason why strays have to be humanely destroyed. Give three other reasons.

5 What is the main point being made by the graph? What do you think can be done about this?

Read these two poems written by a boy and girl at school.

KINGDOG!

A lean dog, a mean dog,
Monarch of the bins.
I do not feel a blow or kick
As the lapdogs do.

They cringe on their rugs
And do tricks for their food.
I hunt and scavenge
And steal for myself.

Beware all you dogs of me 'the King'.
Snarl at me and I'll crush your bones
With my jaws and razor sharp teeth
And you'll snarl no more.

IT'S THE HARD WAY FOR ME

It's a hard life being a stray.
There's never a kind word for me,
No brush for my scruffy hair,
No warm basket for my weary limbs.
You will know me when you see me.
I'm the one with missing ear and the drooping tail.
It's the hard way for me.

In your notebook

1   Do you think Kingdog is pitiful, or frightening or both? Give reasons for your answer.

2   Do you think the author is trying to make us feel sorry for Kingdog? Does he have other reasons as well for writing a poem like this?

3   What does 'monarch of the bins' mean? Is he really monarch of the bins?

4   How is the stray dog in 'It's the hard way for me' different from Kingdog?

5   Which of the two would you like to try to look after?

6   What do you think might eventually happen to these two creatures?

7   Each of the three forms—the extract, the graph and the poems—deals with the same topic of stray dogs but each emphasises something different. If we gave each a 'subtitle' they could be as follows:

Extract: 'Strays continue to be a problem'
Graph: 'What the authorities are doing about the problem'
Poems: 'The problems of a stray'

(a)   Do you think these 'subtitles' have been properly attached? Give reasons for your answers.
(b)   Which of the three forms gives us the most FACTS? Give reasons for your choice.
(c)   Which tells us most about what people in general feel about dogs? Give one fact which supports your answer.
(d)   Which says *most to you* about strays? Give three reasons for your choice. Does the form help make the message more clear?

1 Like any other pet, a dog has important needs of his own. A dog must have his needs catered for or he will be unhappy and most probably a nuisance to everyone. Many people get a dog without giving thought to what he needs.

To protect dogs complete this list of items which you might think someone buying a dog should be able to guarantee.

(a) proper food
(b) suitable place to sleep
(c) exercise
(d)
(e)
(f)
(g)
(h) name tag
(i)
(j)

Put an asterisk at the two most important items and say why you have marked these.

2 Suppose you were made dictator for a day and you were drawing up a set of laws which protected the safety and comfort of dogs, *and* took into account the rights of the public, what would your set of laws include?

Put it down like this.

Law No.	Good for the dogs	Good for the public
1 Dogs and owners must undergo proper training at a training centre.	√	√

3   Is your district a good one in which to bring up a dog? Find out about important things like dog training facilities, vet surgeries, how many dogs there are in the district, places for exercise, etc.

(a) Copy this table and complete it.

Points FOR my district	Points AGAINST my district
e.g. Public generally sympathetic towards dogs e.g. Good places for walks	e.g. Mostly blocks of flats e.g. Many strays running loose

(b) Suggest how you could get round any problems your findings show.

(c) Weigh up the evidence and decide whether or not you would advise someone in your district to buy a dog.

4   Work with a partner

Finding homes for unwanted dogs is a challenging problem for those who try to help. Suppose you were helping to rehome unwanted dogs, what do you think you could do to publicise your work? 'FREE to a good home' postcards help. Can you think of other ways?

(a) Add to this list

Postcards in shop windows
Open day at the dog refuge

Sponsored spot on local radio

(b) Make up a short script for a sponsored spot on local radio to try to rehome a particular dog. Remember to include important information about the animal and think about sound effects which would enhance your presentation.

5 'Pets are every bit as useful to people as working dogs are.'
Work with a partner. One of you argues that the statement is true and one that it is false.

Appoint a chairperson from your group.

Read out your arguments to the rest of the class and be prepared to answer their questions.

Invite the class to vote and see which of the arguments wins.

6 The two young people who wrote the poems obviously are touched by the plight of these strays.

Write a poem of your own.

Think about a dog you know well and write a short poem about his habits and characteristics and about what makes him so special for you.

In the class library search out and read some poems about dogs to give you some ideas.

Seaborough International Festival

Listen to this radio report about Seaborough International Festival then answer the questions

A **In your notebook**

Answer these by writing (a), (b), (c) or (d).

1 The first day of Seaborough International Festival is
  (a) August 13th.
  (b) August 3rd.
  (c) July 3rd.
  (d) August 23rd.

2 One of these personalities will NOT be taking part in the festival:
  (a) James McIntosh.
  (b) Joan Hunter.
  (c) Andrew Young.
  (d) Clive Wilkie.

3 Among those appearing at the festival are included
  (a) a landscape artist.
  (b) a journalist.
  (c) a mountaineer.
  (d) a children's author.

4 The main venue (place where things will happen) is
  (a) the walled garden.
  (b) the beach.
  (c) the marquee.
  (d) the stables.

5 The stables have been converted for use by
  (a) craftsmen.
  (b) the string quartet.
  (c) the puppet show.
  (d) the amateur drama group.

6 Children who attend the Teddy Bears' picnic will receive

(a) a buffet lunch.

(b) sandwiches and soft drinks.

(c) a prize.

(d) morning coffee.

For discussion

7 Explain these phrases:

(a) 'all ages will be catered for handsomely'.

(b) 'remembers then and celebrates now'.

8 Why do you think the reporter says about the Teddy Bears' Picnic 'about which, more later'?

9 What is meant by 'light and not so light refreshments'?

10 Why do you think the people of Seaborough are calling it an *international* festival?

11 Do you think the press preview has been written seriously or lightheartedly? Give reasons for your answer.

SEABOROUGH INTERNATIONAL FESTIVAL 1985—WHAT'S ON WHEN and WHERE

GRAND OPENING 10.30 a.m. by IAN LEEMING
CROWNING OF FESTIVAL QUEEN
SPECTACULAR BALLOON RELEASE

	10.00	11.00	12.00	1.00	2.00	3.00	4.00	5.00	6.00	7.00	8.00	9.00	10.00	11.00	12.00
AUG 3		GRAND OPENING (M) refreshments	BUFFET LUNCH (M) with Stringsong		McINTOSH REMEMBERS (M); CRAFT DISPLAY (closes 5 p.m.) (S); RAFT RACE Heat 1 (B)				PUPPET SHOW (M)			BARBECUE (B) or SUPPER DANCE (M)			
AUG 4	CRAFTSMEN AT WORK (S)	COFFEE MORNING (M) Proceeds to Live Aid; PUPPET SHOW (M)	BUFFET LUNCH with Stringsong		BOAT RACE Heat 1 (B) or FILMS (M)						AMATEUR DRAMA Murder at the Vicarage (M); BECAUSE IT'S THERE! Video show and talk by Clive Wilkie Transatlantic Yachtsman (SC)				
AUG 5		COFFEE MORNING (M) Proceeds to Live Aid; PUPPET SHOW (M)	BUFFET LUNCH with Stringsong		RAFT RACE Heat 2 (B)	TEDDY BEARS' PICNIC (B)						BARBECUE (B) or VIDEO SHOW (M)			
AUG 6	FLOWER SHOW (WG); CHILDREN'S BOOK EXHIBITION and SALE	Talk and Autograph session	BUFFET LUNCH with Stringsong		BOAT RACE Heat 2 (B); ARE YOU SITTING COMFORTABLY? Story reading for children (M)				HOUSE PLANTS COMPETITION (WG)		AMATEUR DRAMA Cards on the Table (M)				
AUG 7	VINTAGE CAR DISPLAY (WP); CRAFTSMEN AT WORK (S)	MESSING ABOUT IN BOATS Boat Club Open Day	BUFFET LUNCH with Stringsong												
AUG 8	CRAFT FAIR (M); BOOK SALE (M); PUPPET SHOW (M)	ARE YOU SITTING COMFORTABLY?	RAFT RACE FINAL (B); BOAT RACE FINAL (B); BUFFET LUNCH with Stringsong								FESTIVAL BALL and DISCO (M)				

M = Marquee SC = Sailing Club B = Beach WG = Walled Garden WP = West Paddock S = Stables

From reading WHAT'S ON, WHEN and WHERE

B *In your notebook*

1   Find out how many different attractions there are.

2   Which attraction appears most frequently?

3   Make a list of attractions which are allocated two or more sessions. Select 2 from your list and give reasons why they merit two or more sessions.

4   Which attractions take place on *one* day? Why? Give a reason for each.

5   Which day would provide the best day out for your family?

For discussion

6   Give a mark out of ten to the following and justify why you gave that mark:
  – Provision for children.
  – Provision for those interested in sailing.
  – Provision for teenagers.
  – Variety of activities.

7   The marquee is not used at all on August 7th. Why do you think the organisers planned it this way?

8   Do you think all ages are catered for handsomely? Which activities would you wish to add or remove? Give reasons for your decision.

9   Suggest three alterations you would make to the timetable.

10   How do you think an event like the Seaborough International Festival benefits local people? Can you think of other ways in which the same benefit can arise?

C

1 More and more towns and villages, schools and colleges, these days hold some form of festival or celebrations. Planning these is not easy but it can be good fun.

Take the part of *chief organiser* and plan a three-day festival for one of the following:

- your home district, village or town
- a special event like the Queen Mother's birthday
- the centenary of your school.

Remember some of the events and activities should relate directly to the subject of the festival and some should be provided to please and entertain the people who will visit the festivities.

Here is how to go about it. You may work with a partner.

(a) Choose an event from the list above or find one of your own.

(b) Make a list of events and activities you think must feature to cater for all ages—toddlers to senior citizens—and for many tastes.

(c) Draw up a table of events, times and places. Keep it simple and clear and don't forget explanatory notes.

You will need a large sheet of paper, a ruler, a pencil and a rubber.

2 *Publicity* for an occasion like this is always very important and great thought is always given to *designing* and *distributing* *publicity material*. Usually a *publicity manager* is appointed.

Take the part of *publicity manager* and

(a) Complete this list of ways to publicise the festival.
(i)
(ii) Posters
(iii) Spot on local radio
(iv)
(v)

(b) Design a poster with a simple picture (you can use magazine cut outs) and a brief but exciting slogan to advertise the festival.

(c) Design a bookmark to advertise *one* of the activities, e.g. a craft fair.

(d) Write a short piece for your spot on local radio. Give as much information as possible but do not exceed 60 words. Record your piece on tape for the rest of the class to hear.

Think of a suitable piece of music for a jingle.

(e) Select another item from the list in (a) and write four sentences explaining why the item is in the list.

1 Write about a festival or similar event which you have actually visited. Use the table below to make brief notes.

Name of the festival		
What I liked about it	What I did *not* like	What I would do to improve it
1 2 3 4	1 2 3 4	1 2 3 4

Now, using your notes write three paragraphs about the festival you visited.

2 Almost every town and village has a traditional festival or historical ceremony which they celebrate yearly. Your town probably has one too.

Write a letter to a pen pal describing your local festival or ceremony no matter how odd you think it is.

A great time was had by all

Read this story about Robert who is 14, his brother Tom (10) and sister Lisa (9). The three are on holiday at their aunt's seaside home and Robert is 'in charge' of them.

Their expedition to the beach over Robert, Tom and Lisa turned in at the garden gate of their aunt's house. The two younger ones rushed ahead, pushed open the front door, threw their bags into the corner and headed for the stairs. They wanted to

5   have a quick wash and a quicker evening meal so that they
could get back out with the least delay. This was the big night.
They were going to the fair and being allowed to stay out late.
Their aunt had promised and they had been saving up.

    At the table, Robert, giving every impression of
10   shouldering his responsibilities willingly, began to advise the
others on how best to get through the coming evening.

    'I wouldn't eat too much just now,' he said. 'You'll
probably be buying burgers and candyfloss and ice cream and
what not at the fairground.'

15   Tom nodded vigorously in gleeful agreement and reached
for another cake.

    Robert continued in his 'I know best' voice.

    'I would advise against going on anything too fast or
bumpy at first. You are already excited enough so maybe
20   rolling a few coins and trying to hook a duck to begin with.'

    Lisa made a 'some hope' face at Tom who grinned back at
his sister. The evening meal was finished in record time. The
three put on some outdoor gear, bid their aunt cheerio and
made for the bus stop.

25   By the time they had reached the fairground, Tom and
Lisa's excitement had reached fever point. Lisa skipped and ran
the last thirty yards. Tom plunged his hands into his pockets to
steady his small change as he broke into a run and even Robert
permitted his own step to quicken a little. Still, he halted them
30   at the entrance and went through a kind of pre-action check.

    'Let's see your money! Make sure its safe! It's got to last all
evening so make it spin out! Watch for pickpockets! Try the
sideshows first, they're cheaper, before you try the big stuff! If
you get lost you know where to go and stand!'

35   He has been rehearsing that speech all day, thought Tom
nodding his agreement to each and every order. Lisa, her back
turned, had been gaping all the while at the noisy spectacle of
the fairground, her eyes shining with delight.

    Nearest the entrance were sideshows and stalls, some
40   small roundabouts and a candyfloss barrow. Further on the
real attractions towered over the crowd, rows of coloured
bulbs winking crazily and pop music blaring at full volume.
Tom and Lisa dived straight for the Whip pausing only long
enough to buy a candyfloss. Then the three of them bought
45   rides on the dodgems, the speedway and the big wheel in
quick succession.

Immediately on stepping down from the big wheel, Tom disappeared into the crowd and returned almost instantly brandishing a hamburger which he insisted on waving back
50 and forth below Robert's nose.

'Lovely, eh?' he said. 'Like one? I'll get it for you.' Tom took his money out.

Robert's speedy refusal and feeble promise to have something a little later made Lisa laugh quietly.

55 'Come on,' she said, linking her arm through Robert's. 'Show me how to win a coconut.'

Robert grasped this opportunity to express his opinion that they should now try some of the games of skill at the smaller stalls.

60 'Just so we can say we gave everything a good try,' he explained airily trying his best to sound wise and knowledgeable.

It was all great fun though. In forty-five minutes flat all their money was gone and all three confessed to having had a
65 fantastic time. Robert had three tickle sticks to show for his skill at throwing darts, Tom had a rattly mirror with a blurred pop star on it, while Lisa had a coconut which she had won after enough 30p shots to pay for two larger coconuts at a fruit shop.

'When Mum and Dad arrive at the weekend, I'm going to
70 bring them here,' shouted Tom.

They had even spent their bus fares and were now walking happily home, the sight, sounds and smells of the fair receding in the background.

'We'll take them on the dodgems first,' said Lisa. 'Then . . .'
75 'No! I think candy floss first!' Tom interrupted. 'Then . . .'

Robert silenced both with a wave of his hand.

'This calls for proper planning.' This was a statement from which many more about the thorny problem of visiting fairs were probably going to come.

80 'The speedway first to get things going then ice creams all round. On to the penny falls arcade for Dad then something suitable for Mum, then perhaps the waltzer or the Meteorite if they are up to it. You know, a well planned tour so they get the best out of it, same as we did.'

85 Tom and Lisa looked at each other with their 'Brother, here we go again' expressions on their faces and burst out laughing.

A *In your notebook*

1   Select the words which you think best describe Robert (or think of better ones)

cheerful dull pompous officious kill-joy kind responsible

Say why you have chosen these words.

2   Why did Robert try to give advice to Tom and Lisa?

3   Do you think they listened to the advice? Give two reasons for your answer.

4   Why do you think Tom said 'I'll get it [the hamburger] for you' (line 51)?

5   Why does Lisa laugh quietly at Robert's 'speedy refusal' (line 53) of the hamburger?

6   Complete this list of reasons which might show that Tom and Lisa don't take Robert too seriously.
  (a) Lisa made a 'some hope' face.
  (b) He has been rehearsing that speech all day, thought Tom.
  (c)
  (d)
  (e)
  (f)

7   How do we know that Lisa and Tom are none the less fond of their big brother?

For discussion

8   In the story it says 'rows of coloured bulbs winking crazily'. Do you think this is a good description? Say why.

9   Robert continued in his *'I know best'* voice. Do you think that phrase refers to:
  (a) the way he was speaking on that occasion.
  (b) the kind of person he is anyway.

10 Is Robert a typical big brother in the way he treats Tom and Lisa?

11 In your opinion, what do Tom and Lisa think of Robert as a big brother?

12 Would you like to go on an outing with Robert?

13 Robert has been left 'in charge' of Lisa and Tom. Do you think that kind of arrangement fair to the three of them?
　　What does it take for that kind of arrangement to work well? Continue with this list drawing upon your own experience as well as the story.
　　(a)　A substantial age gap.
　　(b)　Mutual trust among the three.
　　(c)
　　(d)
　　(e)
　　(f)
　　(g)

14 Lisa could have bought two coconuts with the money she spent winning one. What makes people do that at a fair?
　　Have you ever done that? Write a paragraph about it.

The three young people all had a fantastic time at the fair so it must have offered most of what they like.

1　Cast your memory back to an enjoyable visit you made to a fair. Look at this list of things which probably helped make it enjoyable and write a few words and phrases only to describe each.

atmosphere	highly exciting—laughter
sights	flashing lights—milling crowds
attractions	good variety
food	awful but good fun.

Add to the list for yourself.

2　Write three paragraphs about your memorable visit to the fair.

3 'Fun for all the family' is a favourite slogan seen at the fair.
Work with a partner or partners and draw a map of a
fairground which would be 'fun for all the family'.
You will need a large sheet of paper

> pencil
> ruler
> rubber
> coloured pencils.

Go about it like this.

(a) List the various age groups you must cater for

> (i)   toddlers (pre-school kids).
> (ii) children.
> (iii) teenagers.
> (iv)
> (v)

(b) Choose a *site* for the fair

 e.g. urban—wasteland or park?
>   seaside—cliff top or promenade? etc.

(c) List all the attractions and facilities to be included—like
this:

Side shows
Smallest man on earth
Hall of mirrors

Toddlers and children's entertainments
Helter skelter
3 or 4 roundabouts

'Big' attractions
Whip
Meteorite
Speedway

Other facilities
Food stalls
Publicity board

Games of chance
Rolling balls or coins

Games of skill
Darts
Rifles

(d) Make a key using numbers and symbols to explain your map.

e.g. SW = speedway   CF = candy floss
      W = waltzer   H = hamburger stall

(e) Now draw the map using squares, rectangles and circles to represent the various stalls and roundabouts, and indicating entrances and exits.

Think before beginning about where you are going to locate the different things and how

e.g. Small children's entertainments near the entrance?

All big roundabouts together or scattered throughout the fairground?

4 Draw up a price list covering all the entertainments and food stalls. Give a reason for any particularly high price.

5 Hold a discussion and comparison session with the rest of the class to introduce your fairground map and answer questions and criticisms on it.

Your introduction should include explanations for:

(i) site of the fairground
(ii) the kinds of attractions and how many
(iii) the locations of attractions
(iv) the key to your map etc.
Possible questions should cover:
– Why so many or so few of a particular feature
– Safety precautions
– Actual size.

6 Now use your new map and price list.

Suppose you were publicity manager for the fairground and it had not been a good season because of say weather or unemployment, you would be thinking of ways to attract the public. Here is one to try.
Design some 'package tours' of the fairground.

Using your map and the list of attractions you could do it like this:

The £8 value for money package deal for 2 available Tuesdays and Thursdays.

The £8 book of vouchers gets 2 people:

- Any five big rides (normally 80p for 2 people)
- Any 3 games of chance per person (normally 60p for 2)
- 3 games of skill per person (darts, rifle range, coconut shy) (normally 60p for 2)
- Any 3 sideshows (normally 60p for 2)
- £2 worth of snacks and refreshments from foodstalls listed (saving £3.40)

---

7 As you walk through a fair sideshow stall owners often try to persuade you to part with your money. The more skilful they are at persuasion, the more money they make. Here are some of their comments.

  – 'It couldn't be easier.'
  – 'All the kids get a prize.'
  – 'You've never seen anything like it!'

Write down two or three more slogans that you have heard and thought really worth remembering.

Now select one of these attractions:

  a side show   a game of skill   a game of chance

and make a Roll up! Roll up! type speech to a group of people who have been gaping undecided at your particular attraction.

Record your pitch on a cassette and let the others hear it and give you a 'skilful persuader' rating.

Now you see it . . .

Listen to this conversation between two senior citizens, Jackson and his friend Brewster, who is paying him a visit.

A   *In your notebook*

Answer questions 1–5 by writing (a), (b), (c) or (d).

1   The two men have met

    (a) in the street near Jackson's house.
    (b) in Brewster's house.
    (c) in the doctor's waiting room.
    (d) in Jackson's house.

2   'Lose my rag' means

    (a) discuss the problem.
    (b) enter into an argument.
    (c) get angry.
    (d) think the wrong thing.

3   Jackson is concerned

    (a) about the cost of phone calls.
    (b) for his own safety only.
    (c) about kids getting lost at night.
    (d) for the other elderly people.

4   Jackson has not so far telephoned for assistance because

    (a) he thinks others might think he is frightened.
    (b) phone calls cost so much.
    (c) his neighbour is away.
    (d) he hasn't a phone of his own.

5   The visitor thought it best to keep silent for a while because

    (a) he was afraid of Jackson.
    (b) he thought Jackson was going to reveal his real worry.
    (c) he wanted to enjoy his tea.
    (d) he is fed up arguing.

6   Apart from the two friends there are four other groups of people referred to in the story. Name two of them.

7 From what you have learned about old Jackson from the conversation what *sort* of person do you think he is? Are you sorry for him?

Write down some words and phrases to describe him.

8 Why do you think Jackson keeps raising his voice. Give three reasons.

9 Brewster never raises *his* voice in this conversation. Give two reasons.

For discussion

10 Jackson and Brewster have some things in common in their daily lives and in their personal qualities. Can you name some of these things?

11 There are also differences between the two men. Add to this list.

    (a) Brewster lives in a 'better' area (says Jackson)

    (b)

    (c) Jackson is concerned that people think he cannot cope.

    (d)

    (e)

12 Why do you think Jackson keeps responding so angrily to his friend? Here are some possible reasons. Add one or two more of your own.

    (a) Brewster's quiet way irritates Jackson.

    (b) Underneath Jackson is afraid and is trying to cover up.

    (c)

    (d)

Select the two you think most important and give reasons for your choice.

13 Why did Jackson silence his friend with what the author calls an 'all right, all right' motion of his hand instead of saying something?

14 Brewster says to his friend, 'You said your neighbour . . .' but is cut off. What do you think he was going to say? Why did Jackson cut him off?

15 Brewster refuses to be put off by Jackson's angry reactions and persists in trying to persuade him to call for help. Give reasons why Brewster should take this line.

16 The conversation has one clear message for people like Jackson. He should be ready to seek help if needed.

There is another *message* for *us* however about crime in the streets and old people. What is that message?

17 Does the conversation form of the story help bring the *message* home more forcefully?

Read this extract from a security handbook

It is all too easy for thieves and burglars to get on with their work—*and* get off with it. Every few minutes in this country someone is the victim of a mugger or a bag snatcher. Muggers usually prefer to work in quiet areas attacking people walking along. Bag snatchers frequent busy shopping streets and precincts where there are plenty of bags to snatch and crowds to disappear into. Sadly, pensioners are a favourite target. Many of the assaults take place on pension day not far from the post office. The muggers and snatchers lie in wait close by, size up their prey, follow it to a convenient place, and in a few seconds, someone is relieved of a week's much needed money.

House breakings are equally numerous and burglars do not need darkness to do their work. All they need is a window partially open or a handy ladder or a garage door left ajar and they are inside collecting their spoils from dressing table drawers, biscuit barrels and vases because people leave valuables and money in all too obvious places.

Many thousands of pounds worth of goods go missing and much heartbreak is caused every year because things are made easy for the thief.

In your notebook

1   The extract gives us *information* on how the thefts are carried out. Here are some points of information. Add more to them from the extract.

    (a) Muggers prefer to work in quiet areas.
    (b)
    (c) House breakers also work in daylight.
    (d)

2   There is also a clear *warning* about our own carelessness. Write down what you think that warning is.

3   The extract is about giving us *advice*. Write down two other pieces of advice you think should be given to help combat thieves.

4   Put together, the *information*, the *warning*, and the *advice* to make up the *message* of the extract. Write down that message in three short or one long sentence.

5   Having studied and worked with the conversation and the extract, select a title for each from those suggested below.

    (a) The conversation could be entitled:
        – Always phone for help.
        – Crime causes fear among old people.
        – Rely on neighbours.
    (b) The extract could be entitled:
        – Theft is everywhere.
        – They need not get away with it.
        – We could all do more to combat crime.

6   Which of the two, the conversation or the extract, do you think speaks more loudly and clearly about crime in our society.

    Give reasons for your choice.

C This poster is made up of a picture and two slogans. It gives us INFORMATION, WARNING, and ADVICE very clearly in an easily understood form.

Look at it for a while then answer the questions.

1   There are at least three things which make it *very* easy for the thief. Complete the list.

   (a) Bag seems to be left unzipped.
   (b)
   (c)

2   The thief could be anyone. Which of these people is it most likely to be? Say why.

   (a) Someone in from the street.
   (b) Someone who works in the same office.
   (c) Someone who works elsewhere in the building.

3   What do you think the owner of the purse should have done to protect her property?

4   What do you think would be the consequences if this thief were successful?

5   What other steps should be taken in a big office like this to help prevent theft?

6   Examine the poster carefully. Give it a mark out of ten for how well it gives us INFORMATION, WARNING and ADVICE.

Work with a partner

Hearing the conversation gives extra power to its message. *Seeing* the picture on the poster gives extra power to the message.
   With your partner work on (1) or (2).

1   (a) Here is a list of things which present problems and dangers for people. Add one or two to the list if you wish.
       – out too late
       – smoking
       – drugs
       – over-eating
       – careless storage of medicines
       –
       –
       –

(b) Select the one *you* think particularly serious and make up a 250–300 word speech for a local radio spot to alert people to the dangers. Remember to give
   – INFORMATION (to back up your argument)
   – WARNING
   – ADVICE (some simple yet important things to do).
(c) When you have written the speech, side line the paragraphs you think need special emphasis.
(d) Record your speech on cassette and see what the others think of it.

Some hints to help you:
(i)   a mock interview can make the message more powerful.
(ii) raising and lowering the voice is important on radio.
(iii) slowing the speech can help emphasise a point.
(iv) sound effects can be *effective*.

2 (a) Here is a list of things which present problems and dangers for people and animals. Add one or two to the list if you wish.
   – lighting fires outside
   – careless storage of chemicals
   – road safety
   – cycling proficiency
   – safety in water
   – gates left open
(b) Select the one *you* think particularly serious and design a short comic strip type presentation to alert everyone to the dangers. Remember to give
   – INFORMATION (to back up your argument)
   – WARNING
   – ADVICE

You can go about it like this.
(i)   Draw three or four panels as shown on p. 71.
(ii) Above each write a single sentence description of what is going on in the panel.
(iii) Enter a simple drawing in each panel.
(iv) Below write a comment which could be made by the burglar or by someone watching helplessly.
(v)   Cut the panels and sentences out and stick them on to a suitable background.

(vi) Introduce your finished result to the rest of the class inviting them to offer helpful suggestions for improvement.

Burglar looking at open window

He disappears inside

'He never misses a trick.'

'This shouldn't take long.'

Burglar exits with money and candlesticks

Burglar vaults the wall and escapes

'When will they ever learn?'

'Quick on his feet isn't he?'

Now make your own comic strip presentation.

E

BE PREPARED! Would you know what to do?

If you want to help a victim by reporting to the police a mugging you actually witnessed you would need to possess a number of skills, among them

(a) the ability to observe and note detail

(b) the ability to recall clearly.

Complete this list of things you would note then rearrange them in order of importance.

– the time of day

– mugger male or female

– ....

– ....

– ....

– ....

Kinellan Country Park

Listen to this extract from the Kinellan Country Park souvenir guide book then answer the questions.

A ***In your notebook***

Answer questions 1–8 by writing (a), (b), (c) or (d).

1 The family fortune shrank partly because

    (a) Sir William wasted the money.

    (b) the estate was so large.

    (c) the linen trade fell away.

    (d) Sir William entertained friends in a lordly style.

2 Which of these is true?

    (a) the land has both woods and grassland.

    (b) there are no trees in Kinellan Country Park.

    (c) the land is very rocky.

    (d) the land is surrounded by hills.

3 The Thrig burn

    (a) has three waterfalls.

    (b) supplies the House with water.

    (c) runs south from the rocky area.

    (d) runs north from the rocky area.

4 Some of the design features of the main house can be seen

    (a) on the farm buildings.

    (b) on some of the other buildings on the estate.

    (c) on Dumb Meg's cottage.

    (d) on no other building on the estate.

5 Which of these is situated behind the main house?

    (a) the dairy shop.

    (b) the Visitors' Centre.

    (c) the Museum.

    (d) Dumb Meg's cottage.

6 Dumb Meg worked for

    (a) Sir William.

    (b) the estate manager.

    (c) Sir Andrew.

    (d) a master whose name is not given.

7   If you want to see Dumb Meg now you must go to her now ruined cottage

    (a) in the springtime.

    (b) late on a summer evening.

    (c) on the anniversary of her death.

    (d) on the anniversary of her birth.

8   Parties of eight or more qualify for

    (a) special discount tickets.

    (b) free lunch.

    (c) day tickets.

    (d) free parking.

9   There are at least four groups of people referred to in the story. Here are two. Supply the other two.

    (a) The members of staff

    (b)

    (c) The family itself

    (d)

10 There were two reasons for the decline of the Kinellan family fortune. What are they?

11 Name the two historical periods represented in the public rooms of the main house.

12 What advantage for the visitors is claimed from the family always being in residence? Do you agree with this?

13 The story tells of three mysteries. What are they?

14 Name three features or facilities created specifically for the convenience of members of the public.

For discussion

15 Do you think the mystery stories are or are not an added attraction to visitors? Think of a few reasons for and against.

16 Decide which three features of the Park are probably the main attractions for the visitors. Why have you made these choices?

17 Country parks, safari parks and stately homes are now very popular, partially because they provide *organised entertainment*.
   What in your opinion are the main advantages and disadvantages of that kind of organised entertainment? Stay with the example of country parks and make a table.

Advantages	Disadvantages
A full day's entertainment in the one place.	Basically more suited to adults. Usually a good distance away.

Kinellan Country Park

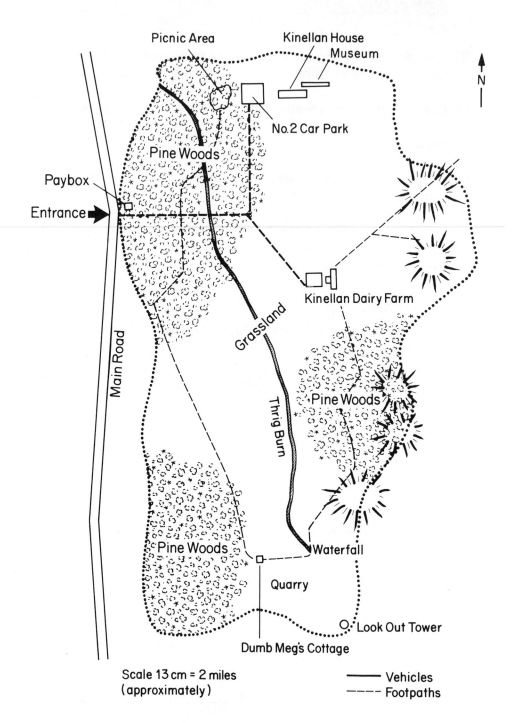

Picnic Area

Kinellan House
Museum

N

No. 2 Car Park

Pine Woods

Paybox

Entrance

Main Road

Kinellan Dairy Farm

Grassland

Thrig Burn

Pine Woods

Pine Woods

Waterfall

Quarry

Look Out Tower

Dumb Meg's Cottage

Scale 13 cm = 2 miles
(approximately)

———— Vehicles
------- Footpaths

Work with a partner

1   Copy this map on to a large sheet of paper.
From listening to the story enter these features:

Quarry   Museum
Kinellan House   Dumb Meg's cottage
Kinellan dairy farm

2   Enter these features (whose locations are not given in the extract) where you think they should be placed. (Be able to give a reason for each choice of location.)

Visitors' Centre   Five Tall Pines
3 car parks   Peacock pen
Deer park   Ring stones
Kiosks   Disused railway
                                     3 picnic areas.

3   Enter two features of your own choice on the map.

(a) One which has a mystery story attached to it. Write one sentence giving a clue to what the mystery is.

e.g. 'It never rains here.'

(b) One which you think would prove an attraction to the public.

4   Study the map and make a list of geographical features which could be included in an interesting walk.

5   There are almost no 'no-go' areas in the Park except places which clearly could be dangerous.
Design a walk which

(a) you would enjoy.
(b) provides a variety of surroundings and safe places of interest.
(c) would take *you* about two hours.

Enter the route of your walk on the map.

6   Design two more safe, interesting walks (one lasting less than 2 hours and one lasting more) which you would recommend to visitors.
Enter the two routes on your map.

7   Name three places on your map where you would put up notices and signs to safeguard the public.

8   We are let in to the story of Dumb Meg, but what about the Five Tall Pines? Can you explain why they are so evenly spaced?

Then there are the Ring stones. How did they so miraculously come to be back in place?

Choose one and make up a short story between you and read it aloud to the class. Be ready to answer their questions.

9   Make up an itinerary for a family day out at the park. Here is how you can go about it.

MORNING Coffee at Visitor Centre		Picnic lunch
AFTERNOON Woodland walk?	Cuppa from a kiosk	
EVENING		Back to the car and home (Fish and chips somewhere on the way)

Enter your itinerary on your map.

10   Make a list of items for sale and other schemes which could make money for the Park. Here are some. Add to the lists.

Items for sale
Postcards
Guide books

Other schemes
Gift vouchers
Adopt a deer
Walking gear for hire

Enter on your map places where these would be available.

11 Put yourself in the place of the country park manager who has to make money for the park.

Think of a suggested tour for a family which will give them an enjoyable day and encourage them to *spend money* in the Park.

12 Again put yourself in the place of the country park manager.

The park is to be extended by about one square mile. The new area extends from a point on the eastern boundary due east of the farm down to a point three-quarters of a mile due east of the Look-out Tower.

Draw the new area on your map and write down the three main characteristics of the terrain of this new area.

Now think of some new activities which could be pursued in this new area which would attract members of the public of all ages. Here is an example. Think of more:

– pony trekking

Above all you must concentrate

Listen to this story about Pamela who is revising for her exams and finds it hard to make any progress.

A   *In your notebook*

Answer questions 1–5 by writing (a), (b), (c) or (d).

1   As she laid out her books, Pamela was surprised that

   (a) she had two hours' homework.
   (b) the living room was free.
   (c) Dad was putting up shelves.
   (d) She had so much homework to do.

2   With the first physics problem Pamela

   (a) thought she did well.
   (b) had difficulty.
   (c) was interrupted by Dad hammering.
   (d) got the wrong answer.

3   When Dad's hammering interrupted Pamela

   (a) she looked up startled.
   (b) she went to see what was wrong.
   (c) she decided to do something else.
   (d) she was working on the second problem.

4   As Mum and her friend chattered

   (a) the baby stopped crying.
   (b) the phone rang.
   (c) Pamela sighed to make them give her quietness.
   (d) Dad went on hammering.

5   When she answered the phone Pamela

   (a) told the caller that Bill was at the snooker hall.
   (b) asked the caller to phone back in twenty minutes.
   (c) said she would tell Bill about the phone call.
   (d) did not tell the caller where Bill was.

6   Eight different people are referred to in the story. Who are they?

7   The story says 'in readiness for two *tedious* hours' homework'. What is the meaning of tedious?

8   Pamela was interrupted a number of times. Write down three of them.

9   That evening, we are told, Pamela had altogether four pieces of homework she could have done. Physics was one. Name the other three.

10   Pamela refers to Mum's friend as her *'noisiest* friend'. The friend does something to confirm this. What does she do?

11   Taking everything into consideration, do you think Pamela could have expected to get two hours' peace to do her homework?

12   What is Pamela's essay to be about? Why does she think it is going to be the easiest essay she has ever done?

For discussion

13   The rest of the family seem to be inconsiderate to Pamela. What do you think they could do to give her a better chance?

14   'Only two more bashes and the job's done,' Dad said in his DIY voice.
    (a) What do the letters DIY stand for?
    (b) What do you think is meant by 'DIY voice'?

Is there a DIY fanatic in your house? Tell the others about what he or she does and what the results are like.

15   The word 'hardworking' probably describes Pamela well. Think of three more words which accurately describe the kind of person she is and explain your choice in each case.

16   The phrase 'the whole house seemed to go mad' is exaggerating things a bit but probably helps the reader to enjoy the story and sympathise with Pamela's plight.

Does the following phrase work in the same way? Give reasons for your answer.

> 'The two women fell to chattering, simultaneously it seemed to Pamela, about the momentous affairs of supermarket life.'

Can you think of two more such phrases in the story?

17 What do you think of Pamela's solution? Is it practicable or is she just dreaming?

18 Why do you think the author wrote a story about Pamela having trouble getting peace to do her homework?
Do you face similar problems? What do you do about it?

B

1 Pamela's evening has gone badly wrong. This can happen whether it's a matter of doing homework or something else. Write about how an evening once turned out differently for you from what was planned. Here is how to go about it.

- (a) Write a *sequence* indicating what you had planned. For example: quick bath and hair wash; best things on; pinch Mum's expensive perfume (or Dad's aftershave); out to meet someone; walk; etc.
- (b) Say where things began to turn out differently.
- (c) Write another *sequence* showing what actually happened then.
- (d) Say whether you were pleasantly surprised or disappointed and why.
      If you were disappointed say (now that you have been through it) what you should have done to avoid the disappointment.

2 Pamela says 'I'll convert the attic'.
Is there a room or a place in your house (or a relative's house) that you would dearly like to convert to make a *special room for yourself?*
Use these headings to complete an account of how you would carry out your project.

- (a) What is your main reason for wanting a special room? (hobby? privacy?)
- (b) Name the place. (For example, corner of the attic, basement.)

(c) On a large piece of paper draw a rough plan of how it looks now.

(d) Make a list of the most important changes you will make (paint and decorate? etc.).

(e) Make a list of what you intend to put in the room (table? desk? bed? lamp?)

(f) Try to show how much it would all cost.

Now a plan of how it is going to look

(g) On another large piece of paper draw a plan of the finished project.

(h) Introduce your project to the rest of the class in the form of an illustrated talk using your two plans and giving plenty of detail. Be ready to answer their questions and receive their advice, especially on *cost*.

3 Suppose you wanted to convert a room for yourself or even change to another bedroom, your parents might take a bit of persuading and you would need to have a good argument ready. Saying 'Oh, you should see my pal's room' would probably not help at all.

Make up a really strong argument for making a change. These headings will help. Write a few notes under each.

(a) Things AGAINST my present room (noisy, expensive to heat, etc.)

(b) Things FOR my new room

(c) Things I could do BETTER in my new room (homework, etc.)

(d) 'It will cost hardly anything' (same furniture—well mostly, etc.)

Once you have your argument ready, ask the teacher to play the part of the stubborn unsympathetic parent and try to persuade her to agree to your plan. See what the rest of the class thinks.

4 'You must concentrate' is very much more easily said than done. Even in a quiet room, minor noises interfere with concentration.

Imagine you are in a quiet room trying to work or sleep or just relax. Leaving aside noises like neighbours, traffic, etc. make a list of the smaller noises which are always there. Indicate which ones you find *irritating* and which you find *comforting*.

5   What do you need to help you concentrate? Suppose you opened a shop selling AIDS TO CONCENTRATION, name some of the items you would always keep in stock.

6   In our story Pamela's family is not being considerate BUT they have their lives to live too.
     Can you draw up some rules for the family to follow so that they give Pamela the best chance to get her work done? Here is an example.
     (a) Noisy DIY jobs should be done at weekends.
     (b)
     (c)
Now draw up some rules for Pamela to try to follow so that she does not impose on her family, and you might end up with a COMPROMISE which would work.

7   Can you suggest any really long term solution for someone in Pamela's position?

Pictures speak louder

ETHIOPIA FAMINE APPEAL

Help!

Christian Aid's emergency help to Ethiopia's famine victims is getting through—nearly £2 million already this year.
Can we keep it up? Only if you can. We need more money urgently. Now. Please.

Christian Aid
PO Box No 1, London SW9 8BH
The churches in action with the world's poor

**Study this ETHIOPIA FAMINE APPEAL poster carefully
and answer the questions.**

1   (a) How many words appear on the poster?
     (b) The printed part of the poster gives us INFORMATION
         and makes an APPEAL.

        (i)   What is the information?
        (ii) Write down the words of the appeal.

2   Look at the picture of the relief workers handling the sacks.
Why have we been shown this picture and not one of starving
people?

3   In short, this poster is trying to say to us 'Your help is
working, but we need more.'

     (a) Give the poster a rating from 0 to 10 to show how well
         you think it is doing its job.
     (b) Do you think the printed message could be more
         powerful? If you do, select *one* of the sentences and
         rewrite it in your own way.
     (c) Can you suggest any changes you would make to the
         picture to make it 'speak more clearly' to us?

Work with a partner

Read these statements which were taken from an information
pamphlet about donation of blood, then do the assignments
which follow.

1   People in good health are needed.

2   Giving blood does not take long and is painless.

3   You may be able to register as a regular blood donor.

4   Thousands of lives are saved yearly by blood donors.

5   Each donor receives a badge.

6 You might need blood some day.

(a) Select the statement which shows most clearly the great importance of giving blood.

(b) Think about making a poster about giving blood. What would make up a poster which had IMPACT? Here are some hints.

(i) Select *any two* of the statements to go on your poster.

(ii) Make a short list of what else should go on your poster, e.g. illustration, addresses, etc.

(iii) Consider this statement made by the proprietor of a picture magazine:
'Tell it in pictures and make it shocking.'

(c) If you wish you should now make the poster using a large sheet of paper, cut outs from magazines, coloured pencils, etc.

Something for yourself

1 Write down the issue or cause in which you are passionately interested. This list may help you:

- Starving children.
- Animals used in scientific experiments.
- Organ transplants.
- Vaccination against childhood diseases.
- Violence at football games.
- Pets to keep old people company.
- Fostering children.

2 Write a 50–60 word personal statement telling why the cause means so much to you.

Now do 3 *or* 4.

3 Bearing in mind that posters are for giving INFORMATION, WARNINGS, ADVICE and making APPEALS and usually contain words and pictures, make up your own poster to draw attention to your cause.

4 Put together a five minute television appeal for your cause saying why you support it. Remember television is for hearing and seeing so think of an anecdote and visual aids to support your appeal.

Work with a partner to see which of you is the more persuasive.

Here is a list of worthy causes. Choose one each (or find one of your own):

– Organ transplants	– Adopt a hungry child
– Donor cards	– Care for the elderly
– Vintage cars	– Dogs for the blind
– Public libraries	– Historic buildings
– Adopt an animal	– Cancer research

Collect newspaper cut-outs, pictures and posters and prepare a talk in an effort to convince the rest of the class that your cause is by far the more worthy, and should get their one pound donation. Think of as many tricks as you can to convince the audience. Deliver your talks and see which of you gets the most one pound donations.

Many young people collect stickers. Some are decorative and shimmer or glow in the dark. Others are pictures of pop stars and many a school folder has been greatly improved by a camouflage of pop star stickers. In public places you will see stickers carrying warnings like 'You are entering a no smoking area'.

1 Make a list of stickers you have seen in use under these categories

FUN	SERIOUS	ADVERTISING

and say what their message was.

2 Particularly effective are the stickers sometimes seen on ambulances. Here are three.

DO US A FAVOUR... STOP SMOKING.

DO US A FAVOUR... WEAR A SEAT BELT.

DO US A FAVOUR... DON'T DRINK AND DRIVE.

Draw three more stickers in the DO US A FAVOUR series and say where they should be displayed.

Button badges are meant to show your support for something. Some people claim that the badges say a great deal about the people who wear them. Do you agree or not?
Write 6–8 sentences stating your case.

Cyclops

Read these two evening programme line ups for STV then answer the questions below.

TUESDAY		FRIDAY	
6.00	**Scottish News** and **Scotland Today**	**6.00**	**Scottish News** and **Scotland Today**
6.35	**Crossroads**—a dramatic day for the hotel—bad news and a surprise.	**6.30**	**World Worth Keeping**—nature films from around the world—you've seen it all before.
7.00	**Take the High Road**—every time Will tries to put something right something else goes wrong. **S**	**7.00**	**Albion Market**—more anonymous phone calls!
7.30	**Name that Tune**—Lionel Blair with a bevy of new contestants.	**7.30**	**We Love TV**—is Gloria competing with Noel Edmonds? Their programmes have a lot in common.
8.00	**Stunt Challenge '85**—6 competitors—4 men and 2 women—some breathtaking stuff.	**8.00**	**South of the Border**—Yorkshireman Edgar Rowley (Brian Glover) reluctantly moves south to live where these strange people seem to be enjoying themselves.
		8.30	**Play Your Cards Right**—points could make prizes for 2 more competitors.
9.00	**Travelling Man**—return of a highly popular series. Former drug squad detective continues the search for his missing son around the canals of the north west. ORACLE SUBTITLES	**9.00**	**Drummonds**—the school is threatened by scandal. **D** ORACLE SUBTITLES
10.00	**News at Ten** and **Scottish headlines**	**10.00**	**News at Ten** and **Scottish headlines**
10.30	**First Tuesday**—an investigation into the explosion at a Lancashire waterworks and survivors of the Battle of Arnhem talk about the tragedy of the airborne landing.	**10.30**	**International Athletics** from Brussels.
		11.00	**Miss Universe**—the beauties from all over the world compete in this well loved form of TV entertainments.
11.35 to 12.30	**Mysteries of Edgar Wallace** Quite a good whodunnit with a corpse and stolen paintings to add tension (black and white).	**12.30 to 12.35**	**Late Call**

A   *In your notebook*

1   How many hours viewing are available on each evening?

2   Some 'programme types' have been entered with initials

   e.g. *Take the High Road*   S (= Soap opera)
          Drummonds   D (= Drama)

Use this set of abbreviations which indicate 'type of programme' and enter an appropriate one against each programme.

N = News, S = Soap, GS = Game show SPEC = Spectacular, D = Drama, Doc = Documentary, R = Religious, TH = Thriller, C = Comedy, Sp = Sport, F = Film.

3   How many hours are given to these types of programmes each evening?

Complete this table.

	N	S	GS	C	R	D
Tuesday Friday						

4   The TV evening has two parts:
   – Early evening extends from 6.00 to 9.00.
   – Late evening extends from 9.00 to the end of viewing.
   (a) In which part are Game shows screened? Give reasons why.
   (b) In which part are Dramas screened? Give reasons why.

5   Name a programme which is screened in the early evening on both days.

6   Name two programmes available in the late evening on both days.

7   Soap operas appear in the early evening. Why?

8 On the Friday evening, the shorter (½ hour programmes) are screened early and the longer (1 hour or 1½ hours) are programmed later. Why do you think this should be?

9 The NEWS occurs regularly at 6 p.m. and at 10 p.m. Why should it have a fixed time like this?

10 Apart from the programme *titles* how can you distinguish between the TUESDAY list and the FRIDAY list?

For discussion

11 Soap opera appears three times over the two evenings. It must be popular. What makes soap opera so popular?
Select one well known TV SOAP and identify four or five features of it which make it so popular.

12 Take these three headings ENTERTAINMENT, INFORMATIVE, EDUCATIVE and discuss among yourselves which of the Friday programmes would fit each category. Always say why.

13 Most of the programme entries are accompanied by a few programme notes. Look at the late evening programmes for both days and give each set of notes a rating out of ten indicating how much they tell you about the programme content.

14 Select the one you think tells you most about the programme content and explain why you gave it such a good rating.

15 Which one tells you least? What would you add to it?

16 Which one set of programme notes would make you want to view the programme?

17 Why do you think the game shows are usually only ½ hour long and the drama one hour?

Work with a partner

1　Good programmes seem often to come on just at the wrong time. Try your hand at timetabling.

- (a) Select a TV programme you both like—you may invent one if you wish—and write some programme notes for it.
- (b) Think of two programmes which appear regularly.
- (c) Plan a *part only* of an evening's viewing and timetable your selected programme in to it along with the other two to make an enjoyable 1½ to 2 hours' viewing.
  Think about these points:
  - (i) Timing is very important since people may have other things to do.
  - (ii) Preceding and succeeding programmes can have an effect on the one in between.
  - (iii) Who is our programme for?
  - (iv) What is on competing channels at the same time?

2　Videos are now very popular—most homes have one—but many lie unused for weeks at a time. Why should that be?

Complete this list of the ways in which a video can be useful.

- (a) You need not miss a programme because you are out.
- (b)
- (c)

3　Balanced viewing for many people would include

ENTERTAINMENT programmes—comedy—game shows.
INFORMATIVE
programmes—news—weather—interviews.
'EDUCATIVE' programmes—documentaries, historical series, nature programmes.

- (a) Find copies of *Radio Times* and *TV Times*.
- (b) Look at what is available on the TV channels for three nights making a quick count of types of programme.
- (c) You are going off on holiday for a few weeks to a remote place which has no TV but has video facilities. Taking programmes from all four 'real' channels make

up your own CHANNEL 5 which will provide you with 12 hours (two full evenings) BALANCED VIEWING.

4   Pretend you own a business which rents out TV sets, videos and tapes and also has for hire 'viewing packages' made up of selected programmes to provide *balanced viewing*, for a variety of groups of people.

Look through the *Radio Times* and *TV Times* for a week and put together a package suitable for these groups:

(a)   A family of five including: Dad and Mum, a boy aged fifteen, a girl aged 10 and Grandad newly retired. (Package must not exceed 8 hours viewing.)

(b)   Ten convalescing men and women who view in a hospital common room (up to 10 hours viewing).

(c)   A class of 28 11 year old boys and girls away for two weeks at a school camp (up to 15 hours viewing).

5   Nowadays films first shown in the cinemas reach the small screen it seems earlier and earlier. *Superman III* made in 1983 was shown on TV in September 1985.

Many people are addicted to watching old movies from the 30s and 40s and video record them avidly. What do you think of cinema films coming to TV? Do they gain or lose something? Are some better on the small screen than on the cinema screen? Do some need the large audience to make them enjoyable? What advantages and disadvantages are there for the public in cinema films being on TV?

Think of *one* film you have seen in both places and make up your mind whether it is a Good Thing or a Bad Thing that it was repeated on TV.

6   Read these two TV crits.

(a) We were treated this week to the first episode of *South of the Border* a new sit com in which Yorkshireman Edgar Rowley moves south to live. He is reluctant to go despite the fact that everywhere around him pits, factories and mills are closing. Brian Glover of wrestling, Royal Shakespeare Company and wholemeal bread fame, gets the part of the loud bewildered Rowley who hasn't had a new suit or an original idea since Yorkshire was invented and seems proud of it. Edgar frequently blesses his dead wife (whose name he actually forgets) and laments the passing of good solid Yorkshire names and values.

I laughed all through the all too short half hour while Edgar's daughters (one an old spinster he says) supervise the removal of the furniture. Episode 2 can't come too soon.

(b) Yorkshire and Yorkshiremen everywhere should be ready to storm the studios of YTV in revenge for the portrayal of a Yorkshireman presented in *South of the Border*. This new series was sitcom at its worst. Edgar Rowley, played overloudly by Brian Glover, is ignorant, prejudiced and dated. He apparently hasn't a brain anywhere and is completely without original thought. He is at odds with his two daughters, one a dried-up old spinster (he says), the other a flibberty gibbet.

We are supposed to have a treat in store as Edgar moves south because pits, factories and mills are all closing in his home county. (It is a pity that Edgar Rowley's mouth did not close with them.) My hope is that Edgar and co. *will* move south and disappear somewhere down the M1.

They disagree completely with each other, but each will be read by people who agree with what is said.

(i) (*For discussion with a partner*) What do you think of the crits?

(ii) Work with a partner and select a TV programme, if possible a new one, which you have both seen.
    Separately, without letting the other see what you are doing, write your crit. saying what you think of:
– the main character.
– one other character.
– the situation (e.g. a surgery, a hotel, etc.).
– the basic idea behind the series.
Now compare notes with your partner.

7 At £58 per year the colour TV licence is good value for money but some people, especially pensioners, find it a struggle to get the money together.

Appoint a chairman among yourselves and discuss this statement:
'TV licences should be free to pensioners and here's why.'

The right choice

Read carefully the *notes on the family* and the *two advertisements* then answer the questions.

The MacDougals
Bill and Irene MacDougal have been happily married seven years now and as yet have only one child, Fred, who is an active three year old. They live in a one-bedroomed flat on the outskirts of a large town. Bill is in a good steady job with fine prospects and has just received a substantial promotion to workshop foreman, no mean achievement for a man of 29. Irene works at home doing typing work for several local firms and this provides a welcome extra income. Working at home enables her to plan her actual working hours to suit family

needs, like managing the household and spending time with Fred. The family circle is completed by Osbert, a chummy beagle, which Bill bought when he was single.

Bill's hobby is running—he runs 6 or 7 miles daily and Irene plays squash and badminton with some of the girls she used to work with.

The couple have been giving very serious thought recently to moving to another house since they can now afford to and after reading house advertisements for ages have decided to investigate two particular places thoroughly, a flat near the city centre and a cottage in a village a few miles away.

LITTLE HENTON, 1 Church Lane

Offers over £35,000

Most attractive semi-detached stone-built cottage in a very desirable quiet, semi-rural area.

On lower floor: front porch, small vestibule, hallway, lounge, living/dining room, kitchen, toilet.

On upper floor: 2 double bedrooms (with Eziglide fitted wardrobes), bathroom and shower unit.

Solid fuel central heating. Good sized, well stocked flower and vegetable garden. Timber garage.

Viewing 10.00 a.m.–5.00 p.m. daily.

---

28 Victoria Terrace

Offers over £31,000

Ground floor flat, in much sought after residential area minutes from the railway station and convenient for the city centre. This flat, part of a tasteful conversion of a town house, consists of entrance hall, spacious lounge, fully fitted kitchen/dining room with built in oven and hob and plumbing for automatic washing machine, bathroom with coloured suite, 2 bedrooms, study/bedroom. Gas central heating. Carpets and curtains included in the sale.

To view contact Milligan, Milligan & Spiers, Albert Street.

A *In your notebook*

The cottage at 1 Church Lane

1 What do you think is meant by the phrases

(a) 'very desirable area'.
(b) 'solid fuel central heating'.
(c) 'well stocked' (garden).

2 The advertisement gives us only *essential* information.
There are some facts which the couple might want to know but
which are not given.
  Complete this list of things you think they would want to
know.

(a) Was the cottage recently built?
(b)
(c) Public transport?
(d)
(e)
(f)

The flat at 28 Victoria Terrace

1 There is quite a lot of information given in the
advertisement but the couple might want to know more.
Complete this list of things you think they would want to know.

(a) Heavy traffic nearby?
(b) Public transport?
(c)
(d)
(e)

2 What do you think is meant by these phrases:

(a) 'much sought after residential area'.
(b) 'convenient for the town centre'.
(c) 'tasteful conversion'.

B *For discussion*

1 Name at least four features which the cottage has but the flat does not.

2 Name at least two features that the flat has that the cottage does not.

3 From the family's point of view write down three advantages which probably arise from the cottage's semi-rural setting.

4 From the family's point of view write down three advantages which probably arise from the flat's urban setting.

C

From what you know of the family and from studying the two advertisements make a *provisional judgement* on the suitability of the flat and the cottage. Select one of these.

– The cottage is poor/fair/good/very good.
– The flat is poor/fair/good/very good.

D

The MacDougals read the advertisements and asked themselves questions similar to those in A, B and C.

Bill said, 'I like the look of that flat,' while Irene said, 'Doesn't the cottage sound good?'

Bill grinned, 'We can afford either one. Let's go and see them!'

They did just that and gained some interesting new information.

Read it carefully.

The cottage

1 The area around the cottage was very beautiful with many attractive walks.

2 The cottage was nearly 100 years old but in sound condition.

3 Two of the rooms needed decorating.

4   The kitchen needed to be renovated.

5   The garden was in excellent condition.

6   The timber garage was brand new and enormous with a handy workshop area.

7   Buses went only twice daily into town.

8   Little Henton village school was 100 yards away.

The flat

1   The area around the flat contained several busy main roads and crossings.

2   The railway ran along behind the house.

3   The rooms were large.

4   The decorative order was excellent.

5   Resident parking with permits was available.

6   Excellent public transport.

7   Upstairs flat was vacant.

8   No garden and the park was two miles away.

Now, with this extra information, and knowing the family's needs, try to make a final judgement on the suitability of the two places. Select one of these.

   – The cottage is poor/fair/good/very good.
   – The flat is poor/fair/good/very good.

The MacDougals bought the cottage. Do you think they did the right thing? Give reasons for your answer.

By choosing the cottage, Bill and Irene MacDougal will come against some problems which will affect their pockets and their daily life. Name at least three of these problems and suggest how they can be overcome.

1 Some people say that living in the country is better than living in the town. Some say the opposite.

   (a) Which do you favour?

   (b) *Work with a partner*.

One of you make up a strong case for living in town. The other make up a strong case for living in the country. Collect your arguments like this.

Town	Country
Good selection of shops and you can shop around for reasonable prices	Could be miles to a shop Must have own transport.
Country	Town
Plenty of fresh air Slow pace of life	Pollution by traffic Rat race

   (c) Present your arguments to the rest of the class either on tape or as a live presentation and see which one of you gains the greater number of votes.

2 Advertise your own house (or an imaginary house) for sale. Go about it this way.

   (a) Give the address of the house for sale.

   (b) State the price you want.

   (c) Give the number of rooms and say what each is.

   (d) Make a list of special features or extras which you think make the house desirable. The list has been started for you.

     Carpets and curtains
     South facing

     . . . .
     . . . .
     . . . .
     Put an * at the five most important.

   (e) Give information on how to make enquiries.

Take a piece of blank paper and set aside a space at the top for a drawing or photo of your house.

Underneath arrange the various pieces of information so that you finish with an attractive and informative advertisement.

Remember you are allowed only 100 words to describe the rooms and the special features and extras.

3 Here are some of the people and agencies to which a person can turn for help when he or she wants to buy a place to live.

- An estate agent.
- A building society.
- A solicitor.
- A surveyor.
- A bank manager/ess.

What can you find out about what each does? Write some questions for an interview with one of them. Your questions should cover

- What his or her day to day work entails.
- The service offered to the client
- A particular piece of work he is engaged in at present.
- A thorny problem he had to solve.
- Whether he or she likes the work and why they chose that job to do.

4 Suppose your family moved house to a place six or seven miles away, what would it mean for you? Write down some information under these headings.

- (a) What I would miss.
- (b) What I would be glad to get away from.
- (c) What I would have to give up.
- (d) What I could continue with.
- (e) What big changes would take place in my day to day life.

5 The cottage is in a *very desirable* area according to the advertisement. What, in your opinion makes an area or district desirable? Make a brief list under these headings:

AMENITIES

For the children	*For grown ups*
e.g. Playpark	e.g. Sports ground

ENTERTAINMENTS

For the children   *For grown ups*
e.g. Saturday cinema club   e.g. Pubs

Make a brief list of services under these headings:

HEALTH/WELFARE   EDUCATION   TRANSPORT

6 Look at the lists and think about your own district. Give it a rating out of 10 to indicate how desirable a district it is.
What would you suggest could be done to improve the rating?

7 Here is a house with 'elastic rooms' arranged for two adults and two children. The idea is that you can select the size of the rooms before you move in by pushing the interior walls back and forth or introducing or removing a wall. Arrange this house as follows:

(a) To suit your own family, *or*
(b) To suit a young couple with two children and a gran. (Remember not to let the rooms become too small. About 3 metres by 2 metres is a small bedroom; 5 metres by 4 metres is a reasonable sized lounge for 4.)

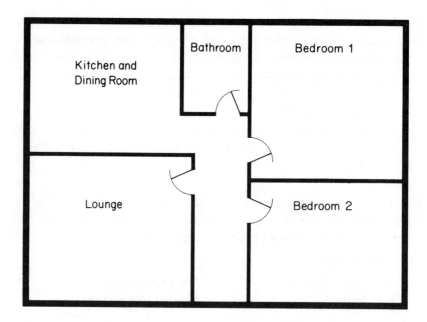

A worthy cause

Read the news report then answer the questions.

I have fidgeted my way through many a council meeting,
glancing frequently at the clock and wishing heartily that it was
all over. Not so last month! Last month's meeting, open to the
public, was the most absorbing and interesting evening I have
5   spent in the hallowed chambers of City Hall. The issue—what
to do with Braithwaite's Mill—had been left aside meeting after
meeting, wrongly so in my opinion, because it generated lively
argument and clearly has been of the utmost importance to
more than one group.

10   Braithwaite's Mill, first operational about the middle of the Industrial Revolution when it turned out linen second to none, closed in 1910. It reopened in 1915 to produce material for uniforms for the Great War and closed again in 1920. It lay empty until the outbreak of World War Two when it was
15   pressed into service to produce aircraft parts and other armaments. Its open loft structure lent itself easily to different manufacturing processes. However the end has now come and a demolition order by the Council was prepared in August. Little did the council know the furore that would raise!

20   Last month's special meeting was attended by several groups who only agreed on one thing—that something had to be done about the Mill. The historical society argued vigorously that the exceptional condition of the Mill only supported their view that a project should be funded to turn it
25   into an industrial museum. The Mill had always drawn visitors in the past and in a transformed state would soon become a paying propositon. Conservation and profit! How about that?

At the hint of money being made available the home owners' group claimed that we should look forward and
30   develop rather than look back and conserve. The Mill, they said, would be ideal for conversion into flats for owner occupation. Many linen mills, notably in Scotland, now served as excellent reasonably priced accommodation.

This idea suited Councillor Sugden who saw new jobs in
35   the offing.

From the chair, the Finance Convenor said that no money *was* available and what the city needed was to earn some. This motivated a member of the public to put in his twopenny worth.

40   'I'm only Joe Public and a jobbing joiner,' he said with the measured thoughtfulness befitting his profession, 'but I say we sell it stone by stone to the Americans. They bought London Bridge and paid sweetly for it. Why not Braithwaite's Mill? I've looked it over and it'll need more doing to it than we can
45   afford.'

The recreation officer pointed out that a recreational complex was desperately needed but that on an issue as important as this the opinions of all of the citizens should be sought, not only those of the people at the meeting.

50   We at the paper agree and we did just that. We canvassed public opinion on the fate of Braithwaite's Mill through street

interviews lasting 3 days, with surprising results. When asked
what they thought, many ordinary citizens shrugged, either
because they did not care or because they felt resigned to the
55 fact that no one would listen to what they had to say anyway.
Who said life round here was dull?

A   *In your notebook*

1   What is the meaning of these words as they are used in the
report?

(a) generated	(line 7)
(b) operational	(line 10)
(c) furore	(line 19)
(d) resigned	(line 54)

2   Find the word in the story nearest in meaning to the words
and phrases below.

(a) forcefully.
(b) truly outstanding.
(c) completely changed.
(d) prompted.
(e) suited to.
(f) sought.

3   Explain the meaning of these phrases as they are used in
the report:

(a) open loft structure	(line 16)
(b) paying proposition	(line 27)
(c) look forward and develop	(line 29)
(d) from the chair	(line 36)

4   Three *groups* of people are represented in the report:

A: the historical society.
B: the home owners' group.
C: the citizens.

Put A or B or C in your notebook to show which of the three
groups would probably make these statements.

- Places to live are more important than industrial museums.
- Why bother asking me?
- Interest in history can be profitable.
- It can fall down for all I care.
- The future is more important than the past.

5   In their reports journalists often use words and phrases designed to make readers sit up and pay attention. For example: 'Not so last month!'
Find three more such journalistic phrases in the report.

6   Find one example of an opinion in the report.

7   Find one example of a biased point of view in the report.

8   At the meeting, what was the effect of the historical society's statement that 'a project should be funded'?

For discussion

9   What do you think must have happened in the previous months to make the council order the demolition of the Mill?

10   What must have happened to cause a special public meeting to be called to discuss the fate of the Mill?

11   What do you think should be done with Braithwaite's Mill? Why?

12   Do you think conserving buildings and places from the past is a good thing? If so, list the ways in which 'conservation benefits us'.

13   'I say we sell it stone by stone to the Americans.'
Is that idea as potty as it might sound? Say why you would be for it or against it.

14   The Americans did buy London Bridge and reconstructed it stone by stone in the Arizona desert. What, do you think, made them undertake such a gigantic operation?

15 It could be said of this newspaper account that it is a bit 'smart' and is impertinently 'taking the mickey' out of a serious discussion.

Select from these words to indicate what you think of the report (or supply your own word):

pleasing, irritating, amusing, serious, noteworthy.

Explain your choice by quoting words or phrases from the report.

16 Do you find the attitude of the ordinary citizens surprising? Explain your answer. Do you know of anything similar which happened near where you live?

17 What does the phrase 'with the measured thoughtfulness that befits his profession' tell us about the jobbing joiner.

Why should the reporter use that phrase?

B Often people with clipboards and ball-point pens will come to the door or stop you in the street and ask you to answer some questions about a product. This is called market research and is a very useful way of getting information back to the manufacturers.

1 Have you ever been interviewed by a researcher? What happened? Write two paragraphs about it covering:

- where the interview took place.
- what the product was.
- the kinds of question asked.
- what you thought of the questions.
- whether you enjoyed the chat.

2 Perhaps you have done some market research and taken part in interviewing people. Write two paragraphs describing one interview you can remember well. Say whether or not you enjoyed it.

3 Saving Braithwaite's Mill is a *worthy cause*. Is there a similar *worthy cause* in your district. It might be one of the following worthy of restoration

- a church
- a disused cinema with the distinctive 1930s architecture

- a vintage vehicle in dreadful condition
- a canal
- a famous person's house

(or anything else you choose).

Select one of these and describe the predicament it finds itself in now. Plan your description out like this.

- Say what the item or object or building is.
- Say what its present condition is.
- Explain its fate if it is not saved.
- State why you think it should be saved.
- Say what you want (money or help) from the public.
- List a few ways in which everyone will benefit if the object is restored.

4   Now, pretend that you are helping a group of people to save and restore a cinema. Draw up a questionnaire of six questions to find out what the public thinks. The questions should cover:

- whether the public knows about the cinema.
- whether they are aware of the danger it is in.
- if saved what it should be used for.
- raising money.
- gathering support recruiting helpers, etc.

Number your questions neatly and think of an easy way to record your answers.

5   You and your group have just been given permission to publicise your worthy cause at the park on a Saturday afternoon.

Select your worthy cause from this list.

- Give the kids a games park.
- Save the playgroup.
- Don't let Hercules (a much loved work horse) be put down.
- Save _____'s house or street—it's living history!

You are allowed:

(a) To set up a stand and a small display.
(b) To sell flags and other items.
(c) To ask passers by to complete questionnaires.
(d) To address passers by.

(e) To play appropriate music in an orderly fashion.

(f) To collect money.

(g) To design and display two placards.

Select three of the above and describe what you would do to fulfil each one.

6 Free speech is everyone's right in this country. In big cities like London and Edinburgh you will regularly see people addressing a crowd on a pet topic, sometimes to the pleasure of others sometimes to their annoyance. Have you ever seen this? Where was it? What do you think of it?

Write two or three paragraphs describing the episode and your feelings about it.

7 *Work with a partner*

Everyone has a 'hobby horse' which they get on to whenever they can. It could be health foods, the dangers of smoking, lady drivers, equality of treatment for men and women, etc. What is your hobby horse?

Suppose the two of you got a ten minute slot at a regular open air 'Speakers' corner', what would you do to present your cases forcefully? Think of dress, visual aids, how to be heard by all, etc. Write down the main points of your speeches and deliver them with all your might and powers of persuasion, as far as possible 'off the cuff'.

Each class member is allowed to 'donate' a pound (an imaginary one, of course!) to only *one* speaker, so do your best to get those pounds for yourselves.

8 Sometimes people call at the door and try to engage you in discussion about religious matters like faith and belief. Do you think they should be allowed to? Explain your point of view.

Day by day by day

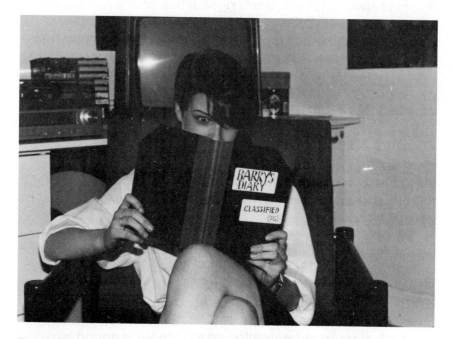

Read these entries from Barry's diary then answer the questions.

MONDAY October 21st

Maybe I'm one of those people who get moody when Autumn comes along or maybe today wasn't a good day, moody or not.
    The downstairs dog wakened me at 6.20, the 3rd time in 3
5 days. I decided to get up and make the best of things. Monday again! School again! Why 5 days out of 7? That's over 70% of the week! Talking of school, the bus was crowded again, mainly with those screaming primary pests. Why can't they get a bus of their own? Nice surprise at school, I must admit. Mr
10 Sawers took ill at 10.00 and had to go home. The student took his place and did much better. Still she's young—he's old. I wonder if she will get to be like him once she's put in a hundred years at the chalk face.

The head boy visited to make the monthly announce-
15 ments. One more win on Saturday and the first XV will have
had an unbeaten season so come along and support, etc. 7
aside finals tomorrow against AUGIE'S. Must go. Why can't we
just get a good noticeboard and save the poor guy a lot of stair
climbing and cat calls. A lot of homework tonight. I was
20 'promised' 2 hours nightly by fourth year. I did 2½ tonight and
its only 3rd year. Maybe time should go backwards.

TUESDAY October 22nd

Had a good night's sleep and I felt great when I got up! Perhaps
weeks should all start on a Tuesday. Good fun in Physics (4th
25 and 5th) *and* at last I can make sense of strobes! Had a great
time at games. Couldn't do anything wrong!! I caught and
kicked something fantastic and just put my head down and
charged! Mr Pertwee said it was great to see me galvanised
into action (I must look it up!) and showing healthy aggression.
30 (If I remember rightly, that's the kind of thing Mr Sawers
warned us against.) If I keep it up he said I could soon see my
name up on the fixture board! The post-game showers were
cold as usual but it doesn't matter to a player in top form!
Went straight over to Augie's after school for the
35 seven-a-sides. We all shouted and screamed ourselves hoarse!
Just as well I write my diary and don't go in for audio tapes like
Jennifer Pickles. Dad thought it was great news about my
prowess at rugby. He even offered to give me something
towards new kit! (I wonder what I can do to get him to give me
40 something towards a MUSIC CENTRE—there's a great offer at
Dixons!) Mum just said that I should wrap up warmly for rugby
if I'm going to get all hoarse like that!
End of a good day and it's only Tuesday. I think I'll play my
David Bowie tape in bed. Isn't the 'slumber' setting a great
45 thing!

WEDNESDAY October 23rd

A funny thing happened on the way home. I hope I never see
this again. I was in McLuskey's looking through the tapes and
records and things. I got the 3 blank tapes offer and was
50 walking towards the door when a rumpus got up. A man
(assistant manager I found out later) suddenly stood against
the street door barring my way and told me to stay where I

was. Just then, a boy about 12 began running about among the aisles and counters, faster and faster. Somebody must have
55 tripped him up because he went sprawling and threw something away across the floor. A panda car stopped outside and two policemen came in and the next thing I knew the boy was being taken away to the back of the shop. But that's not all. The assistant manager said I could go but he told me to turn
60 out my pockets first and show him the receipt for the tapes. I couldn't find it! I looked everywhere again and again. I had slipped it absent mindedly into my breast pocket. The assistant manager waved me out! I nearly *passed* out. My skin crawled with fear all the way home!
65   I'd better not forget the rest of today.
     Bucketing with rain this morning and no school bus. I wonder why. After waiting about half an hour a lot of people went home but Bert and I jogged the distance because we didn't want to miss physics. Somebody must have phoned the
70 school because nobody said a word when we arrived soggy at 9.45. By eleven o'clock I was wishing I had gone home. We had C and A 3rd period and even though I tried to be invisible I was put to play the part of a market stall owner shouting out about his wares! Talk about embarrassed! Bert giggled and Jennifer
75 P closed her eyes! I'm just not suitable for it. You would think anyone could see that!
     Physics was good. Mr Pepper let us use the strobe kit! (If I'm lucky my eyes will recover in 7 days!)
     Monday was dull. Tuesday was good fun. Wednesday has
80 been startling! First, no bus. Then my noteworthy dramatic debut (I spell that d.e.b.a.c.l.e.) then that horrific episode at McLuskey's. I think I'll put my light out and get an early night.

A   *In your notebook*

1   Why do you think Barry refers to the children as screaming primary pests?

2   Give a reason of your own why the primary pests can't get a bus of their own.

3   What do you think AUGIE's (line 17) is short for?

4   Explain the meaning of the phrase 'chalk face' (line 13).

5   Why does Barry say 'A hundred years at the chalk face' (lines 12–13)?

6   Why does Barry put inverted commas around 'promised' (line 20).

7   Can you explain these words and phrases?
   (a) '7 a side'   (lines 16–17)
   (b) '4th and 5th'   (lines 24–5)
   (c) 'slumber setting'   (line 44)
   (d) 'C and A'   (line 72)

8   What would it mean if Barry saw his name up on the fixture board?

9   How would you know that the school is a good distance away from Barry's home? (2 reasons)

10   What kind of store do you think McLuskey's is? Give reasons for your answer.

For discussion

11   Barry writes as if everyone will easily understand his abbreviations and his own special brand of language.
   Find three examples of this 'special' language from the diary.

12   What do you think of Barry's statement 'Nice surprise at school, I must admit' about Mr Sawers taking ill?

13   Describe Barry's mood at the end of Monday. Has he alone brought this mood upon himself?

14   Can you understand Barry's momentary bafflement with the phrase 'galvanised into action'? Say why.

15 What do you think of Barry's statement 'It doesn't matter to a player in top form'.

16 Why do you think Mum told Barry to wrap up warmly for rugby if he was going 'to get all hoarse' (line 42)?

17 Barry uses no less than twelve exclamation marks in Tuesday's entry. Why does he do that?

18 Barry says 'I'm just not suitable for it. You would think anyone would see that!' Does it strike you as curious that he says this?

19 Why does Barry say 'I spell debut d.e.b.a.c.l.e.'?

20 He ends Wednesday by saying 'I think I'll . . . get an early night'. Why does he say this?

Work with a partner

1 Although diaries of all shapes and sizes are on sale, some people prefer to buy a fairly plain notebook and enter the dates for themselves. Can you add to this table of PROS and CONS.

You can use an ordinary notebook and make a diary	
PROS	CONS
Cheap Looks 'real'	You have to organise it for yourself

2 Find an ordinary school notebook to make into a diary.
   (a) Write down at least three things you would do to improve its appearance.
   (b) Describe how you would prepare the pages for writing on, e.g. Dates? Why? No dates? Why?
   (c) Make a frontispiece to introduce the diary.
   (d) Enter some forthcoming events.
   (e) Write up the first page.

3   When Barry was in McLuskey's he seems to have witnessed the arrest of a shop lifter. It clearly took Barry by surprise since he had never seen such a thing before.

Has anything of the kind happened to you?

Write a short piece along these lines to describe what happened.

- (i) Where you were.
- (ii) What you were doing at the time.
- (iii) What made you realise that something was happening.
- (iv) A brief description of how the incident itself began, went on and ended.
- (v) What part if any you played in it.
- (vi) How you felt afterwards.

If the incident were to happen all over again, would you behave differently?

4   *Work with a partner*

Five days out of seven each week might, on the face of it, look a long time to spend at school.

- (a) Work out the true number of hours we spend weekly at school.
- (b) Work out the *average* hours of homework you do weekly.
- (c) Add (a) + (b) together and calculate the percentage of the week given to school or school studies.
- (d) Can you design a better school week plan which would
  - (i) guarantee adequate study time;
  - (ii) guarantee adequate free time; and
  - (iii) be a notable improvement on what we have now?

5   *Work with a partner*

Some people like keeping a diary because they can record large amounts of information in a factual yet individual personal way. The special thing about diary entries is that they are unique.

Make a list of four events which have occurred over the past school week.

Now, separately, without consulting each other, write a short paragraph about each event to go into a diary.

Once you have finished, read each other's work to see how differently, and thus how individually, you have recorded the event.

6   Barry writes 'C and A', '4th and 5th' 'Augie's', etc.
Draw up a list of words and phrases which make up the special vocabulary of your school.

7   The purpose of a diary can also be to look forward.
   (a) Write down the names of the next six months.
   (b) Copy this table into your notebook and enter one or two events under each category for each month.

Month	National events	School events	Family/ personal events
1			
2			
3			
4			
5			
6			

   (c) Put ** at the *most* important events in each category. Put * at the important events.
   (d) Which column was easiest to fill up? Why?

8   An appointment diary looks quite different from a personal diary.
   (a) Write down as many people as you can who might need an appointment diary.
   (b) What do you think the pages of an appointment diary look like?
   (c) Now find an appointment diary and study it. Do you find anything surprising about it?

Questions for listening passages

1 A sporting offer

Listen to the passage then write the answers to these questions in your notebook.

1   Write down 2 words or phrases that tell you that the story takes place in the morning.

2   Name 3 items of cricket gear on offer.

3   Apart from their price, write down one other attractive feature about the trousers.

4   Write down 2 pieces of important information you find on the side panel of the packet.

5   Barry sounded hopeful that he could get the money together to buy the cricket gear. Why was that?

6   He did not sound quite as hopeful at the end of the story. Why?

2 Rules! Rules! Rules!

Listen to the passage, a discussion between Pamela and Susan, and answer the questions in your notebook.

1   Which items of school uniform is Pamela wearing when she meets Susan?

2   Write down one thing that is against the school rules at Pamela's school.

3   Write down one thing in the school rules (apart from wearing a uniform).

4   Why does Pamela always do her homework?

5 Write down something Pamela says which might show that not very many pupils wear school uniform at her school.

6 Write down 2 things Pamela said to her Dad to try to persuade him to rent a video.

7 Give one reason why Pamela thinks school uniform should not be worn.

3 Letter to the editor

Listen to the passage then answer the questions in your notebook. Put T, F or DS to show TRUE, FALSE or DOESN'T SAY for questions 1–5.

1 There is something every day in the paper about the Wareham Street district.

2 Wareham Street used to be a much better place.

3 The only remaining shop tries to provide all of the local people's needs.

4 The houses still in use need many improvements.

5 There have been more than 50 arrests for drunkenness and glue sniffing.

6 Wareham Street looks depressing. Write down 2 things from the story which show this.

7 Jack Aldersley thinks the local people *do* have money to spend. Write down 2 of the things he says they spend it on.

8 Aldersley is *very* critical of the Wareham Street people but he does show some sympathy. Give *2* facts from the story to show this.

4 Weekend in the wilds

Listen to the passage from Barry's diary then answer the questions in your notebook.

1 What 3 things made Barry 'bone weary'?

2   Name the 4 members of the McLeod family.

3   What did Tom bring with him when he joined Barry at the loch?

4   Barry's family and Tom's family used to live near each other. Give one fact from the passage which might prove this.

5   Complete this list of things Barry did after tea on Friday.

  (a) Went to the loch with the children to skiff stones.
  (b)
  (c)
  (d) Returned home.

6   Write down one fact from the story which seems to show that the kids were enjoying Barry's company on the Saturday morning.

7   What 2 things took place in the early part of the evening at the rescue team meeting?

8   Supply the missing parts of this sequence:

  (a) The team member climbed to the top of the frame.
  (b)
  (c)
  (d)
  (e) The victim sat up and grinned.

9   What do you think was taking place with the team member falling from the frame?

5 The visitor

Listen to the passage then answer the questions in your notebook.

Put A, B, C or D to show your choice of answer.

1   The lawn with the landing pad was situated

  (a) at the rear of the building.
  (b) at the front of the building.
  (c) between the forest and the mountains.
  (d) to the west of the building.

2   The story tells us that the mountains

  (a) lay about ten miles away.
  (b) were very rugged indeed.
  (c) lay beyond the forest.
  (d) surrounded the lodge.

3   The landing pad was situated

  (a) well away from the lodge.
  (b) among the trees.
  (c) immediately outside the french doors.
  (d) so that it was hidden from the lodge.

4   The story tells us

  (a) that the helicopter frequently arrived at the lodge.
  (b) that it was making a surprise visit.
  (c) that it had come for the first time.
  (d) none of the above.

5   When the helicopter landed

  (a) the soldier saluted and waited.
  (b) the visitor stepped down from the cockpit.
  (c) there was a pause.
  (d) the pilot began to check the engine over.

Answer 6, 7 and 8 with T, F or DS to show TRUE or FALSE or that the story DOESN'T SAY.

6   The action takes place in the early part of the day.

7   The officer was ready and waiting for the arrival of the helicopter.

8   The conversation which took place outside the lodge was unfriendly.

9   The pilot apparently remained in the helicopter. How do we know this?

10 Clearly the visitor was taking no chances as he arrived. Give 2 facts from the passage to confirm this.